Praise for How to Start Your Business for Entrepreneurs

D0175827

'Robert Ashton has done it again and the timing is perfect. He covers all the key topics around starting a business in a practical and comprehensive way, with lots of tips, case studies and apt quotations. All you need.'

GEORGE DERBYSHIRE, CHIEF EXECUTIVE, NFEA

'What Robert Ashton doesn't know about entrepreneurship isn't worth knowing. Unlike other authors who are all about theory rather than practical advice, Robert gets straight to the point of what it takes to start and run a successful business.'

DAN MARTIN, EDITOR, BUSINESSZONE.CO.UK

'This book is grounded in real world experience. Robert Ashton has a rare gift for simplifying complex subjects and making them fun and easy to apply. Action your learnings and enjoy your results.'

IAN CHRISTELOW, MANAGING DIRECTOR, ACTIONCOACH

How to Start Your Own Business

For Entrepreneurs

How to Start
Your Own
Business

For Entrepreneurs

Robert Ashton

PEARSON
Prentice Hall
BUSINESS

Harlow, England • London • New York • Boston • San Francisco • Toronto • Sydney • Singapore • Hong Kong
Tokyo • Seoul • Taipei • New Delhi • Cape Town • Madrid • Mexico City • Amsterdam • Munich • Paris • Milan

PEARSON EDUCATION LIMITED

Edinburgh Gate
Harlow CM20 2JE
Tel: +44 (0)1279 623623
Fax: +44 (0)1279 431059
Website: www.pearsoned.co.uk

First published in Great Britain in 2009

ISBN: 978-0-273-72358-5

British Library Cataloguing-in-Publication Data
A catalogue record for this book is available from the British Library

Library of Congress Cataloging-in-Publication Data
Ashton, Robert, 1955-
 How to start your own business for entrepreneurs / Robert Ashton.
   p. cm.
 Includes index.
 ISBN 978-0-273-72358-5 (pbk.)
 1. New business enterprises. 2. Entrepreneurship. 3. Small business--Management.
I. Title.
 HD62.5.A817 2009
 658.1'1--dc22
                              2009018041

10 9 8 7 6 5 4
13 12 11

Text design by Design Deluxe
All cartoons © Jurgen Wolff
Typeset in 9/13pt Swis721 Lt BT by 30
Printed and bound in Great Britain by Ashford Colour Press, Gosport

Contents

Part Four Managing your business

Part Five Looking ahead

...for Entrepreneurs

Being an entrepreneur can be the path to controlling your own life and to financial success. With the *For Entrepreneurs* series, it doesn't have to be a lonely journey any more. Our expert authors guide you through all phases of starting and running a business, with practical advice every step of the way. Whether you are just getting started or want to grow your business, whether you want to become a skilled marketer or salesperson or just want to get your business finances under control, there is a *For Entrepreneurs* book ready to be your experienced, friendly and supportive business coach. Our titles include:

→ *How to Start Your Own Business for Entrepreneurs*

→ *How to Grow Your Business for Entrepreneurs*

→ *Selling for Entrepreneurs*

→ *Marketing for Entrepreneurs*

→ *Book-keeping and Accounts for Entrepreneurs*

You'll find more information and more support on our website: **www.forentrepreneursbooks.com**.

Jurgen Wolff, General Editor

About the author

Robert Ashton has started three businesses and sold two. He works with entrepreneurs of all kinds, advising growing businesses, social enterprises and evolving charities.

He is a popular and entertaining business speaker and TV presenter. He writes for a number of business and consumer magazines. This is Robert's ninth book.

Robert would love to hear from you if you think he can help you become more successful. You can contact him by email at **Robert@ RobertAshton.co.uk** or via his website at **www.robertashton.co.uk**.

Also by Robert Ashton

Achieving Business Alchemy (2002), Hodder & Stoughton

Copywriting in a Week (2003), Hodder & Stoughton

How to Sell (2004), Hamlyn

The Entrepreneur's Book of Checklists (2004), Prentice Hall (Second edition published by Prentice Hall, 2007)

The Life Plan (2006), Prentice Hall

Teach Yourself Life at 50: For Men (2007), Hodder & Stoughton

I Know Someone Like That (2008), Turnpike Farm (Foreword by Stephen Fry)

Instant Entrepreneur (2008), Prentice Hall

Acknowledgements

No author can write a book alone. I am very grateful to the many business owners, advisers and professionals who have shared so much of their knowledge and experience with me over the years. This book is as much a distillation of their experiences as it is of my own.

In particular, I would like to acknowledge the very practical support of Dan Martin and the team at BusinessZone.co.uk. As well as providing a wealth of online information that readers might find useful, they have more than 40,000 registered members, all real business owners like you will soon be.

In fact, most of the case studies in this book tell the stories of members of ukbusinessforums.co.uk, the sister website of BusinessZone.co.uk, where members meet and share ideas. I was spoilt for choice when I invited members to tell me their stories. My thanks go to each enthusiastic volunteer.

Finally, it is both traditional and appropriate to thank the team at Prentice Hall. You are only reading this book because they have worked hard to produce and promote it. They are very selective and very professional – and, above all, great fun to work with.

Introduction

There is something magical about the birth of a business. It's very like becoming a parent. The sense of awe and wonder that you have created something new will amaze you. If you're already a parent, you'll know what I mean.

Like a baby, your new business will need your constant care and attention. It will be completely dependent on you for its welfare and safety. Oblivious to danger, your new venture will need a healthy supply of cash, either from investment or customers. This book will show you what to do.

As your business grows, its demands on you will change. In fact, like a growing child, it will steadily develop and mature. Eventually, if you have reared it well, your business will become self-sufficient able perhaps to support you now without your day-to-day involvement.

Creating your own enterprise presents a wider range of options than starting a family. Just as all babies have very similar needs so, too, do businesses. The difference is that not all businesses are the same. You might be planning to build a global empire, or just develop an interest into a part-time business that fits around your other commitments. Although the basics will be the same, the scale and detail will be very different.

Businesses also grow at different rates. A part-time enterprise can take years to develop, while a company established to exploit a particular opportunity or piece of new technology might, of necessity, grow very fast.

It doesn't matter what your entrepreneurial aspirations are – this book will help you to make your business journey. Use it to nurture the seed of your business idea. Use the tips it contains to grow your enterprise and, importantly, learn from the experience of those who have already made the journey.

Before you start

Part One

See your future as an entrepreneur – crystal clear

Chapter One

You've decided to start your own business. You have a good idea and now want to turn your dream into reality. Inevitably your vision will not yet be crystal clear. There will be doubts, concerns and many questions. Let's work on your concerns, answer your questions and help you gain an insight into your future as an entrepreneur.

How do entrepreneurs see the world?

To the experienced entrepreneur, the world is full of opportunities and challenges. The opportunities are there to be evaluated and perhaps exploited. The challenges are merely obstacles to be overcome.

Both are greeted with enthusiasm and a positive attitude. The seasoned entrepreneur appreciates that pitfalls are inevitable and that success is always achieved at a price. The skills an entrepreneur develops over time enable them to:

→ see the opportunities that others may miss;
→ remain rational under pressure;
→ make objective, thought-through decisions;
→ never take setbacks personally.

Small opportunities are often the beginning of great enterprises. DEMOSTHENES

How to Start Your Own Business for Entrepreneurs

Over time you, too, will acquire these skills. This book will help you until you do.

Case study
Emma Jeffery, The Project Portal,
www.theProjectPortal.co.uk

Emma Jeffery is an example of someone who is attracted to the entrepreneurial life. Setting up a website for a construction company as part of a student internship inspired Emma to seek a career in web design. Initially she worked part-time, earning enough to fund the completion of her degree.

Other factors influencing her decision were the low set-up costs and being able to work from home in the evening. It fits well with her other life as a student.

She has prepared a business plan to keep her on track and set up the systems she needs to operate her enterprise. When she graduates she will have more choice than most: to use her experience to get a good job or to build up her own enterprise. For Emma, entrepreneurship means choice.

How entrepreneurial are you?

The good news is that you are entrepreneurial. Why else would you be planning to start a business? The challenge is to work out exactly how entrepreneurial you are. Or, to put it another way, how can you structure your ambition and your enterprise to best suit your personality and style?

We are all different, and it's important from the outset that your business gives you every opportunity to focus your efforts on what you do best. Equally, you need to appreciate what you might find less comfortable and make sure you don't create a business you won't actually enjoy.

Here are some questions to ask yourself. There are no right or wrong answers; nor are they questions that demand a yes/no answer. We need to work out where your greatest entrepreneurial strengths lie.

How competitive are you?

Some people just have to win at every opportunity. Others are simply content to take part. The more competitive you are, the more likely you will welcome the cut and thrust of business life. If, on the other hand, you are not competitive, you will probably have decided to start a business where it's less important to do marketplace battle with rivals.

COMPETITIVE PEOPLE

Are usually good at:	May not be too good at:
Goal setting	Attention to detail
Selling	Listening
Self-motivation	Losing

Remember that there is a lot more to business than being competitive. Your business does not have to be the best, just good enough.

How intuitive are you?

Intuitive entrepreneurs can sense what has to be done and when. They are usually pretty good at reading their marketplace and, in particular, at understanding exactly what their customers are expecting of them. If intuition is not one of your strengths you may need to work harder to measure what your customers are feeling about you.

INTUITIVE PEOPLE

Are usually good at:	May not be too good at:
Reading a situation	Believing market research
Picking up good and bad vibes	Asking obvious questions
Trusting and following their instinct	Justifying their actions

The more intuitive you are, the more likely you are to try things that have not been tried before.

How sensitive are you?

One of the first lessons you will learn as your business becomes established is not to take criticism personally. It is possible for somebody to have the highest regard for you and absolutely no interest in your business. Equally, you need to be tough enough to take rejection. Any business that wins every deal is not trying hard enough!

SENSITIVE PEOPLE

Are usually good at:	May not be too good at:
Responding to feedback	Accepting criticism
Motivating people	Giving negative feedback
Adapting	Sticking to their guns

How determined are you?

Determined people don't give up. They keep on trying after others have walked away. Sometimes determination is enough to win through, although, on its own, it is rarely enough. People who lack determination often accept the status quo and will find easy routes to success.

DETERMINED PEOPLE

Are usually good at:	May not be too good at:
Finding ways to overcome adversity	Taking no for an answer
Championing their business	Bending to meet customer needs
Remembering to do things	Knowing when it's time to move on

How economical are you?

It's always good to be careful with money. Starting and growing a business presents countless opportunities to invest in the useful things. The economical entrepreneur will spend frugally, buying only the things they really need. Someone more used to spending their money as fast as they earn it will find it harder to be economical.

ECONOMICAL PEOPLE

Are usually good at:	May not be too good at:
Borrowing things	Making investment decisions
Buying well	Encouraging customers to buy more
Avoiding waste	Maintaining quality

As a new entrepreneur you will be competitive, intuitive, sensitive, determined and economical to a greater or lesser extent. Probably you will also find that the business you are planning to start fits you and your personality. For example:

→ very competitive people often sell or distribute things;

→ very sensitive people often provide caring services;

→ very intuitive people often start consultancies.

Danger!

Structure your new business to suit your natural personality and style. Work with, not against, the person you are.

Toolkit

How well do you know yourself? There's a really useful online self-assessment questionnaire at **www.create-a-life.co.uk/assessments/ know_me.html**.

Case study
Gary Ennis, NSDesign, **www.nsdesign.co.uk**

Gary Ennis is a good example of how to align your personality and skills with your business. He set up NSDesign in 1999 and has grown the business to a team of five. They form a one stop shop for businesses seeking to promote and sell online. Gary attributes his success to his determination never to forget the customer. 'However good you are,' he told me, 'unless you can communicate with and involve your customer, it's going to be a struggle.'

The decision to start a web business was not lightly taken. Trained as an architect, Gary was lecturing at a local university when the growth of the internet captured his imagination. Already something of a computer expert, he saw that creating effective websites would enable him to combine all his interests and be part of an emerging new industry.

He took the plunge and hasn't looked back once. He loves his work and is proud of what he and his team have achieved; they've twice been shortlisted for Scottish Creative Entrepreneur of the Year, and in 2008 won an 'Outstanding Performing Business' award.

How entrepreneurs set goals

You have set one entrepreneurial goal already. You have decided to start the business. Established entrepreneurs break down every aspect of their enterprise and set goals and targets for each of them.

They will then have a number of key statistics that they monitor closely. These may be calculated for them, then summarised on a single sheet or screen. Many people call this a dashboard because, like a dashboard on a car, it provides important information at a glance.

When you start your new business, you are unlikely to have sophisticated systems that calculate and present this information to you. You therefore need to set and monitor some simple goals. All successful entrepreneurs do this by some means or other.

Long-term goals summarise the very reasons you have started your business. They capture the entrepreneur's vision for the future in a way that enables them to be measured. For example:

→ 'In three years our annual sales will reach £1m and we will be making 15 per cent pre-tax profit.'
→ 'In five years we will have 35 per cent of the local market.'
→ 'In five years we will sell the business for at least £750,000.'

Probably you have set some long-term goals for your business already. It is important that they are both measurable and realistic. In fact, you will need these goals for your business plan, but more on that later.

Short-term goals/milestones are set by entrepreneurs to make sure that the business stays on track. Business growth is not constant. It will often be slow at first, and then accelerate as awareness grows, customer numbers increase and confidence in the product or service builds.

In setting goals, you need to recognise this and plan accordingly. For example, here are some possible goals and milestones:

→ 'Annual sales will be:
  – Year 1 – £200,000;
  – Year 2 – £300,000;
  – Year 3 – £450,000;
  – Year 4 – £700,000;
  – Year 5 – £1,000,000.'

→ 'We will win one new customer a month this year who spends at least £5,000.'

→ 'Our products will be reviewed in six trade journals this year.'

Case study
Gordon

Always a keen gardener, when Gordon was made redundant from the factory where he worked he decided to start a landscape gardening business. He had always done odd jobs for beer money and it seemed logical to make this his new career.

Gordon worked out that to give himself the standard of living he wanted, as well as to afford the best garden machinery, his annual sales needed to be at least £40,000. This meant working for 200 days a year at a rate of £200 a day. To achieve this rate, he knew he had to do more than just cut grass and weed borders.

Gordon decided to target high-earning private householders and offer them a service that included security fencing as well as gardening and a guaranteed daily visit when they were away from home. He would charge customers £2,000 a year for an all-in service.

Case study
Grace

When Grace moved house and could not find a reliable local window cleaner, she decided to do something about it. She knew from her job as operations manager at a busy conference centre that success was all about good customer service.

A door-to-door survey in her neighbourhood showed that her frustration was shared by many others. She started a Facebook group and soon had 200 members, many of whom were suggesting additional household services.

She left her job, recruited three excellent eastern European workers, and launched her business. She plans literally to clean up in North London before expanding her business nationally.

You will find such examples of entrepreneurial activity all around you. However, it's important to set goals for your business that you are comfortable with. Do not try to copy other people.

Working out your business potential

Deep down, most of us know how large we would like our business to grow. Bigger is not necessarily better – although often it is!

As you plan to turn your business idea into reality, there are two aspects of business potential you need to consider – income and value.

Income

The starting point for most entrepreneurs is to work out how much they want to earn, both now and in the future. When you start your enterprise, it will take a while – perhaps months or years – before it gives you the level of income you might be currently enjoying as an employee.

What you need to work out is how much more you can earn working for yourself than you would if you remained employed. Even if you are not currently working – for example, because you are raising a family – entrepreneurship has to stack up financially against the alternative of getting a job.

Factors you need to consider when calculating the income potential of your new enterprise include:

→ the potential market for your products or services;

→ the cost and time involved in setting it up;

→ how much you can do yourself and how much will require staff or subcontractors;

→ how competitors will react to you entering the marketplace;

→ how fast you will feel comfortable growing your business.

Value

Building value into a business is where the experienced entrepreneur can score over the newcomer. Although a successful business can give you a good income and lovely lifestyle, building a business with a view to eventual sale is really the name of the game.

To think about selling your business before it has even started may seem strange. It is, however, vital to create a business that builds value and can, at the earliest possible time, continue to grow without your involvement.

Factors you need to consider when calculating the value potential of your new enterprise include:

→ intellectual property such as patents and trademarks that can be protected;

→ momentum created by an increasing number of customers making repeat purchases;

→ opening up a new market in such a way that a large competitor chooses to buy your business rather than compete with you.

It is also important to realise that your business potential is not limited by your own skills or abilities. You simply have to be able to recruit, motivate and manage people who have the skills, abilities and perhaps contacts that your business needs. It is often said that a good entrepreneur is somebody who hires people brighter than themselves. Just because you want to start a business, it does not necessarily follow that everyone else wants to do so, too. One of the paradoxes of enterprise is that sometimes people prefer to grow a business as an employee rather than have the headache of being their own boss.

Of course, it's also important to learn what you don't know yet. Building your skills builds the potential of your business.

Frequently asked questions

Here are some typical questions asked by people about how to start a business.

Starting my own business looked like a good idea until I checked out the competition. I wonder, do I really have what it takes to be successful?
Self-doubt is natural, and without it we would lack the objectivity to really make a business different from its rivals. Remember that you don't have to be better than anybody else, just different in a way that your customers recognise and value.

Everybody in the world can benefit from using the product I plan to distribute. Am I right in thinking, therefore, that my business has boundless potential and can grow into a major international corporation?
I suspect you are being encouraged to see this huge opportunity by the people whose products you are going to sell. In reality, no business can sell to everybody and you are going to need to focus on those sectors of the community you can relate to or access best. Work out how big your business needs to be to give you what you want and then plan how to achieve that.

I'm only 25. Why would I want to sell my business before I'm ready to retire?
Simple: if you can sell your business for £1 million at the age of 30 then you can invest that money in your second enterprise, which might grow even faster. Look on a business as you might look on a career. Sometimes you will move within your existing organisation, while at other times it is better to cash in and start again.

One of the big questions you may have in mind is how to find exactly the right business opportunity for you. We'll take a close look at that in the next chapter.

Key points

→ As an entrepreneur you have to see the positive in everything.
→ Your business needs to be structured to suit you, not the other way around.

→ Goals need to be both measurable and frequently measured.

→ It's OK to hire people brighter than you, providing you're the boss.

→ Structure your business so it can be sold easily, even if you don't ever sell it.

Next steps

What action will you take to apply the information in this chapter? By when will you do it?

_____

_____

_____

_____

How to find your biggest business opportunity

Chapter Two

Your first business idea may not be your best. Before you start spending money, you need to look at as many options as possible. That way you give yourself the best chance of creating an enterprise that makes you money and is fun to run.

Don't take the bull by the horns, take him by the tail; then you can let go when you want to.

JOSH BILLINGS

The right business for you will:

→ enable you to use skills you already have and about which you are confident;

→ benefit your customers in ways they can easily measure;

→ create the opportunity to do something in which you are passionate.

What is the right kind of business for you?

The relationship you will have with your new business is rather like the relationship many enjoy with a life partner. There are going to be ups and downs, highs and lows, thrills and spills. Giving up and walking away will be both difficult and expensive, so is best avoided. The more careful you are choosing the right business, the more likely it is that you will enjoy more good times than bad, and that the relationship will last and be profitable.

Case study
Jeff

Jeff worked for a large insurance broker, specialising in company pension schemes. In his spare time he restored old cars. He began trading old-car spares on eBay and soon his hobby was earning him a few thousand a year. He decided to take the plunge, leave his job and build a classic car spares business.

When he discussed the business idea with his wife she was less than convinced. She asked him how much he'd make if he simply started his own pensions brokerage. He checked out the commission rates and spoke to a couple of industry contacts.

Together the couple worked out that he could make much more money by selling pensions than from car spares. Six months later he launched his own business as a pensions broker. His income quickly rose and he had more spare cash to indulge in car restoration. He still trades car spares on eBay, but accepts that financial services are where he makes most of his money.

However much you want to do something, unless there's demand you don't have a business – you have a hobby!

Why you'll be more successful if you get this right

No one likes to have their good ideas challenged. Nevertheless, two heads are almost always better than one. In the example above, Jeff might simply have followed his heart and set up the car spares business. This would have:

→ made him less money;

→ perhaps lost its appeal if now a business rather than a hobby;

→ taken him away from his easiest way to make money.

You need to be objective if you are to get this right, not be led totally by emotion. Whatever motivates you to become an entrepreneur, your most important goal is to make money. The more profitable your business, the better able you are to:

→ spend your time doing work you enjoy;

→ invest time and money in the things you consider most important;

→ build a business you might one day be able to sell.

In other words, getting your priorities right means you create a business with the best possible chance of financial success. Profit gives you choice.

When is the right time to work this out?

Clearly you need to decide what business you're going to start before you make any significant commitment. You don't want to lock yourself into any one thing until you're totally convinced it's the right choice for you.

It's important that you look at several options and ideas before making an irreversible decision. It's equally important not to sit on the fence for too long. If you have been made redundant, for example, the longer you delay starting your business, the more of your capital you might have spent on living expenses. You also have longer to wait before your new business delivers income.

The secret is to think before you jump, then jump in a way that is not too restricting. Inevitably your new business will evolve as it develops. You need to make sure you leave room for this to happen.

Danger!

If you suddenly find yourself with a redundancy cheque or perhaps even an inheritance, take a few weeks to get over the shock before making irreversible decisions about a new business.

Some common risks

There are some pitfalls to watch out for when you are starting a new business:

→ Anyone offering you a 'now or never' opportunity. There are very, very few business opportunities that are unique. However urgent making a decision today might appear, it always pays to avoid anyone trying to pressure you into making a decision.

→ Well-meaning advice from people who have no enterprise experience. Friends often tell you about their unrealised business ambitions. Don't get talked into living out someone else's dream.

→ Anything that has never been done before. There's actually very little new in the world of business. As a rule, it's better to improve on what already exists than to break new ground.

Case study
Kate Hanes, Greenfinder, **www.greenfinder.co.uk**

Working as a teacher in Africa, the Middle East and Australia gave Kate Hanes an insight into how green we could be. Always environmentally conscious herself, she had encouraged her friends and family to think green.

'Green living is something that I am passionate about,' Kate told me. 'In the last few years with the climate change issue hitting the headlines it seemed an ideal time to set up a green business.'

Kate was always being asked questions about recycling by friends and neighbours, so it seemed logical to set up a website advising on sustainable living. Kate sells advertising on the website and organises green events to generate income.

Kate's business combines her teaching skills with her knowledge and experience of environmental matters.

Like Kate, the more passion you feel for your business idea, the more energy you will find to drive it to reality.

Exercises to help you work it out

There are a number of factors you need to consider when trying to identify the business idea that will give you all that you are looking for. These include:

→ working out objectively what you do best;

→ deciding what you enjoy doing most;

→ calculating the market opportunity with the greatest potential.

This is very different from reviewing your CV or from performance review appraisals with your boss. You need to consider skills you have developed both at work and at home. A good way to work out what you enjoy doing most is to create a table like the one below. This enables you to rate tasks on a scale from 1 to 5, where 1 indicates that you don't enjoy the task at all and 5 indicates that you enjoy it a lot.

HOW MUCH YOU ENJOY DOING THIS

	1	2	3	4	5
Preparing food					X
Dealing with customers					X
Teaching			X		
Dealing with suppliers			X		
Working in the evening	X				
Being part of a large team		X			
Working alone				X	

The table above was filled in by Kate, a lecturer at a catering college. She used to run a restaurant, but after having children she no longer liked the unsocial hours and so got a teaching job.

You can see, however, that Kate misses food preparation and dealing with customers. She doesn't mind teaching but clearly is no longer motivated by it.

After doing this exercise with a close friend, they came up with the idea of opening a sandwich shop. This would provide the customer contact and hands-on food preparation that Kate was most missing.

However, just wanting to do something is not a good enough reason to actually do it. There has to be a market ready and willing to welcome your product or service. The world is full of businesses established because the owner wanted to do something. Many do not succeed because potential customers do not view the new enterprise with the same enthusiasm.

Checking out your market opportunity so that you do not open a business that nobody wants to patronise is covered in Chapter Three. Here the focus is on you and your personal ambitions and expectations.

What about some alternatives?

Let's continue with our example of Kate the college lecturer considering opening a sandwich shop. Most people, having thought of the business that seems to meet their personal needs, look no further. They simply go out and seek the best place to start the business of which they first thought. But there are always alternatives. For example, Kate's options include:

→ a sandwich shop, either on the high street or in a business area;

→ a sandwich round visiting people at work or even at home;

→ setting up a café inside a large corporate headquarters;

→ a snack foods factory wholesaling to corner shops and filling stations;

→ an event catering company, which would free her from the routine of having to open a shop every single morning.

Your turn

To make sure that you consider all the alternatives, here are three simple exercises that will help you. Remember that, unless prompted, you cannot possibly know what you do not yet know. You have to start with the obvious and then move sideways to create a broader spectrum. Grab some paper and a pen so that you can record your answers.

Exercise 1: who else does that?

In the middle of a piece of paper, write down the principal activity or business idea you have decided is best for you. Next, in a circle around it, write some other businesses that contain the same activities. Then create a wider circle containing less obvious examples. For example, if you started with gardening, your word group might look like this:

Green burials cemetery   *Exhibition floristry*
Propagating house plants   *Market gardening*
Pitch and putt course   **Gardening**   *Herb growing/drying*
Grounds maintenance   *Landscape design*
Rural crafts centre   *Tourist attraction*

Can you see how – by starting with what you want to do – the wider you go, the more options you discover? Each option can then be explored in more detail to see which one offers you the profit and lifestyle you seek. Look beyond the obvious to identify your biggest opportunity.

Exercise 2: where does this happen?

Most people starting a business are going to operate in one particular marketplace. If your customers will visit your premises, this is a physical marketplace constrained by geography. If you're going to supply a specialist service to transport companies, then you might cover the country but only deal with one market sector, say tanker fleets.

Now repeat Exercise 1, but this time looking at *where* not *what*. The example below is by a software developer, brainstorming the types of location or setting where his voice recognition programme might be used:

Vending machines   *Theme parks*

Disability charities   *Security equipment industry*

School computers   **Voice recognition software**   *Office computers*

Leisure industry   *Household appliance makers*

Information kiosks   *Language schools*

This exercise helps you to look outside the industry sectors you already know and understand. It can help you to list the potential markets for your business, ready for you to explore and evaluate in the next chapter.

Danger!

One product or service can have a far higher value in some markets or applications than others. It makes sense to focus on the most lucrative markets first.

Exercise 3: what is the opposite of what I want to do most?

In this final exercise, you need to explore the very things you do not want to do. This is about you – not your skills or experience. For example, you might decide:

→ you hate late nights;

→ you don't think you would enjoy cold-calling;

→ you get bored doing the same thing week in, week out;

→ you like to have the flexibility to take the odd afternoon off.

Then look at the business you are thinking of starting and consider the extent to which it provides the opposite to what you do not want to do. For example:

→ if you hated late nights you would not run a bar;

→ if you don't like to cold-call, you might prefer retailing to door-to-door selling;

→ if you get bored quickly, you want lots of new customers rather than providing the same service to the same customers for many years;

→ if you want flexibility, you don't want to have your diary full of commitments for months into the future.

This exercise will help you to see the impact of the business you are considering on your preferred way of life. It may seem trivial to look at personal preferences in this way, but creating the lifestyle you want is one of the key reasons for starting your own business in the first place.

Frequently asked questions

Here are some of the questions that people often ask when considering what business to start after reading this book.

My partner thinks this is silly and that I should just get a better job. Who's right?
Everyone is different and it could be that what excites you about entrepreneurship terrifies your partner. Make it a challenge to create a plan that reassures even your partner that you are going to succeed.

I have done the exercises in this chapter but the business I really want to start is so specialist, where will I find customers?
The rest of this book will help you to work out how to find customers. What you need to appreciate right now is that the internet will probably help you to do this. More important is to recognise that, in general, specialist business start-ups do better than those that simply try to meet everyone's needs. You're probably on the right track.

I've read this chapter twice and am still short of good ideas. What should I do now?
To trigger your inspiration, take some time off and look around. Visit a town you do not know and look at the businesses there. You will see plenty that you don't

want to copy, but try to build a list that contains elements of the businesses you encounter that you might be good at. Some of the best businesses are started by people who see something being done badly and decide to do it better. You might be one of those people.

I actually now have too many ideas and don't know which to do first! How can I decide?
Listen to your instinct. Which idea does your heart tell you will be the most successful? Also look at which you think will be the easiest to start and which will have the greatest potential. It is important to be focused on just one idea when you come to write your plan.

If you're not sure yet whether you've found the right business, the next chapter will help you to evaluate possibilities in more detail.

Key points

→ Your first idea may not be your best – look around before committing.

→ Listen to those around you, but remember that it is your decision.

→ Be objective and look at all your skills and interests.

→ Don't be persuaded to rush into something that you have not checked out.

→ Exploring the ridiculous can help you find the obvious.

→ Remember that this will not be easy, so take your time and get it right.

Next steps

What action will you take to apply the information in this chapter? By when will you do it?

_____

_____

_____

_____

↑

How to be really sure your business idea will fly

Chapter Three

Probably you have already researched your business idea. But have you covered all the angles? Most people test out their new business idea on family and friends. Their feedback is important but not necessarily unbiased. You owe it to yourself to take an objective look at your business proposition before you fully commit to the project.

 It is the new and different that is always most vulnerable to market reasearch. MALCOM GLADWELL

What research do you need to do?

Market research is a two-edged sword. Too little and you run the risk of investing in a flawed concept. Too much and you can be overwhelmed by conflicting data and never start at all.

As a new entrepreneur, you will also feel an emotional attachment to your business idea. This is a strength in that you have to champion it as you get the enterprise off the ground. It can also cloud your judgement if your research tells you what you really don't want to hear.

The following are some of the things you should research before starting your new business.

Your motivation

It sounds obvious, but understanding your motivation for starting a business is an important piece of research. You are going to acquire customers, suppliers and possibly employees. Each of these groups has to be able to see a value to them in dealing with you. If your sole aim is to make money, you will overlook this important factor. At every stage of the market research process, you must see your enterprise through the eyes of those who will choose to do business with it. Price alone is not enough. There have to be tangible benefits for all.

For example, let's say you plan to open a laundrette in an area where lots of students live. Your motivation is to make money – and you know from your initial research that if enough people become regular customers, it will be very profitable. But there are some major issues to consider before you jump in:

How to Start Your Own Business for Entrepreneurs

- → Your customers are already washing their clothes somewhere. What will you offer that will make them choose to come to you?
- → Your suppliers will be happy only if you succeed. Otherwise you become a liability. How will they be reassured?
- → Working in a laundrette can be tough. The hours are long and the work can be boring. How will you make staff happy?

The happier you make your customers, suppliers and staff, the more profitable your business will become. Don't focus on what you want; focus on what they want.

Market size

How many people already use what you propose to supply? This can be straightforward if, for example, you are going to be a haulier, as you can easily find out the volume of freight shipped by road. If, on the other hand, you are breaking new ground, perhaps providing training to potential stand-up comics, then determining market size is almost impossible. You just don't know how many people fancy themselves as comedians!

Market trends

Many once-big names in industry have disappeared because they continued to supply a declining market. For example, Richard Garrett was a very successful nineteenth century maker of steam traction engines. When diesel tractors came along, the company did not diversify quickly enough and quite literally ran out of steam.

However, your business does not have to be supplying a growing market. Sometimes a declining market can give you as much business as you need, as long as there is little competition. As others diversify away, you remain as a specialist supplier. Thatchers are an example of this.

Market analysis

It is almost impossible to start a business that is unique. Almost everything has been done before or is already being done by others. Your research needs to help you understand who is active in the market you're planning to enter. Specifically you need to work out how you will differ from your competitors. Remember that your customers will largely base their decision to buy from you not on what you do, but on how you differ from alternative suppliers.

In other words

Market analysis describes an investigation of the growth and the composition of a market. It helps you to find out what is happening.

Case study

Roland Schreiber Expresso,
www.expresso-online. co.uk

Roland Schreiber runs Expresso, a popular independent coffee shop in Norwich city centre. He competes with all the major multiple coffee shop outlets and attracts his customers because he is different. He allows artists to exhibit on the café walls, so there is always something new to see. He also serves every cup of coffee with a chocolate wafer in the saucer. Both are small things, but they make the customer experience different enough to attract customers.

How to balance your instinct with market research

Your instinct will give you a good feel for what will work and what won't. But instinct alone is not enough. Before investing money, you will require hard facts and evidence of need for what you're going to do.

Let's assume you are going to open a vegetarian restaurant and you want to find out whether the facts support your instincts. Here's how you could do it:

Your instincts suggest:	Check it out like this:
People want to eat healthily	Look in people's supermarket trolleys
Vegetarianism is gaining ground	Read press and survey reports online
Local restaurants are not vegetarian friendly	Look at menus and ask in a few places why they have such a limited veggie menu
There's a local demand	Ask around and see

The risk of relying purely on instinct is that you are looking to justify your idea. You are seeking out support (which is important) and might not be as objective as you should. But your instinctive research, quick and dirty though it is, will at least allow you to become more comfortable talking to others about your business idea. In particular, talking to people you don't know. It's a short step from selling and therefore important to do.

The 'So what?' game

One way to really test your business idea is to challenge it. You can do this by playing the 'So what?' game. It's basically a conversation with yourself, but it helps to write it down.

Ask yourself a series of questions about your enterprise and answer each with 'So what?' Then go on to justify the idea. It's rather like the way a child won't take no for an answer, simply responding to each point the parent makes with 'Why?' Eventually the parent gives in, but you must not.

Here's an example:

'I'm going to open a vegetarian restaurant.'

So what? Who's going to go there?

'Well, more people are eating vegetarian now – it's so healthy.'

So what? Since when did people choose to do healthy things?

'But it makes sense to be healthy and there's lots of evidence that says that meat eating is in decline.'

So what? You're talking about intellectuals, most won't bother.

'That's as may be, but there is no vegetarian restaurant in this city so what business there is will come our way.'

So what? If there was a demand, there would already be one.

At this point, you should have a few doubts. Is there a market? Has someone else tried and failed? How much of this plan is your personal idealism and how much does it make sound commercial sense? All these are questions to ask yourself as you begin to check out your opportunity.

Quick and easy ways to check out your business idea

The more you research your business idea before starting out, the better your chances of success. However, it is wise to keep a sense of proportion and not get bogged down in detailed statistics.

Time saver

Thorough research now will reduce your marketing costs later.

Here are the key factors to consider.

Market size

You need to be totally confident that there is a market out there for what you are planning to do. That means that people:

→ need what you provide and are currently not supplied with it;

→ buy what you do elsewhere and are likely to change;

→ are not yet 'in the market' but are likely to become interested.

To determine your market size you also need to work out realistically how big a territory your business can service. For example:

→ How far will people travel to visit your shop?

→ How large are the online communities you can service via the internet (and what are the physical constraints that might limit delivery)?

In some markets this will be easy, while in others it will be virtually impossible. For example:

→ an artificial limb maker can access health statistics that accurately predict the number of amputations carried out each year;

→ a maker of snack foods faces a far more complicated exercise as demand is largely stimulated by advertising and the way the products are displayed in supermarkets.

To work out your potential market size, consider all or some of the following activities:

→ Look online for relevant published statistics.

→ Look at the advertising 'media packs' of publications read by your target audience (these usually define market size and state their share of it to justify the rates they charge).

→ Visit the places your target customers go and literally see who's there.

→ Look for online communities frequented by your target customers.

→ Get copies of the annual reports of listed suppliers to your marketplace. These may define market size, and the narrative might also reveal market issues you are not currently aware of.

Market trends

You don't need a growing market to succeed but it helps. All markets are constantly evolving. This is due to:

→ changing user behaviour (e.g. people are buying smaller cars now);

→ fashion (e.g. more men are growing beards);

→ legislation (e.g. public buildings have to be wheelchair accessible);

→ economic factors (e.g. rising metal prices makes recycling more profitable).

These trends might influence your decision about the products or services you are going to market. For example, it's as easy to distribute beard trimmers as electric razors. You might give both equal focus in recognition of the trend towards beard wearing.

To work out how your market is changing, consider all or some of the following activities:

→ Read trade journals and see what's being hailed as new.

→ Visit relevant exhibitions and see what's being promoted.

→ Search online for new patents/technology in your sector.

→ Ask journalists who write about your marketplace (buy them lunch).

→ Talk to academics and researchers working in your market sector.

→ Carry out (or commission) a consumer survey.

Market analysis

Trends show you where a market is going. Analysis helps you to find your place within the marketplace. Inevitably you will be competing with existing providers. You need to balance your understanding of market size and trends against what's already there. From this you will pick out the ways in which you can be different from your rivals.

The way you do this is by looking hard at your competitors. Work out their strengths and weaknesses. How have they become complacent and not moved with the times? What are their specialities and how might yours differ?

Your activities might include:

→ reviewing competitor websites and literature;

→ mystery shopping and buying from your rivals;

→ interviewing your target customers about their buying experiences.

How to Start Your Own Business for Entrepreneurs

Each UK region has an observatory website where public sector organisations publish a wide range of population, economic and other useful statistics. It can really help you to define your market size. To find your local observatory, visit **www.regionalobservatories.org.uk**.

Remember that you want to differentiate yourself clearly from others. This makes marketing easier and helps customers see the value of giving you a try. Sometimes this will mean changing your plan slightly, perhaps specialising in an area you've found is not well covered elsewhere. Conversely, you might simply decide to offer the same products or services as everyone else, but make the customer experience more pleasurable.

For a more detailed guide through the entire marketing process, see *Marketing for Entrepreneurs*, one of the other titles in this series.

Case study

Rochelle Byles, Pootle, www.pootle-shop.co.uk

As a stay-at-home mum and former primary school teacher, Rochelle Byles was very aware of the high price of baby goods. She found that a lot of her friends were searching eBay for cheaper second-hand items. As any parent knows, young children grow out of things very quickly.

However, while the eBay prices were good, Rochelle's friends wanted to see the product before bidding. This put them off actually buying from an auction website.

When her son started school, Rochelle decided to open a shop selling good quality second-hand baby equipment. This would not only help parents looking to save money, but it would also provide a convenient marketplace for those wishing to cash in on things they no longer needed.

She carried out her research locally, talking to lots of other young mums. Everyone liked her idea so she took the plunge and opened Pootle. Word soon spread and the business is prospering.

What your bank manager will want to know

If you need to borrow money to start your business, your bank manager will have many questions. Even if you don't need to borrow money, it's good to behave as if you do. The discipline of preparing your plan for scrutiny by a professional banker is a good one. In fact, you need to appreciate that when a bank manager says no, they might well be doing you a favour. Just as they don't want to lose their money, nor should you be in a hurry to lose your own.

Most banks provide template business plans and lots of other useful tools. These are there to help you, as well as to recruit you as a customer. Most are, by necessity, complex as they have to cover a wide range of situations. Don't be afraid to miss out the stuff that doesn't seem important to your situation (your bank manager will soon tell you if it is!).

Above all else, a bank manager wants to determine that:

→ you understand the business sector you're entering;
→ you have the energy, enthusiasm and determination to succeed;
→ you've done your own research and written your own plan, even if this proves to be just a starting point;
→ your personal financial situation is not too precarious;
→ your family are right behind you and support your plan.

Frequently asked questions

Here are some typical questions asked by people researching their business opportunity.

I've worked in the industry for years and know the ropes. I'm only doing this because my employer went bust. Why do I need to do research?
Well, how about because your employer did go bust! Clearly things were not right and your view of the industry might by undesirably biased by the organisation you've just left. Take a fresh look and see what it's really like.

My business idea feels right. I know there's no one doing it yet, but that's because no one has yet had the courage to stand up and be counted. Isn't that enough to be getting on with?

Beware of becoming a martyr to a lost cause. There's usually a good reason why there is no one already doing something. Often someone's tried and failed, or the marketplace is not ready yet. If you take one tip from this book, let it be that you should always let others be the pioneers and break new ground. You can then follow when it's safe and provide customers with choice.

I have a large redundancy cheque and a small pension. The kids have left home so, really, do I need to do all this stuff? Can't I afford simply to tick along?

Sure, but if you're not in business to make a profit then you're simply taking up a hobby. Take your business seriously and, yes, do what you're going to enjoy, but make sure you're properly rewarded for what you do. Remember, money means choice and you don't know what challenges await you later in life.

In the next chapter you'll find out how to structure your business to help ensure that it will be a success.

Web bonus

At our website, **www.forentrepreneursbooks.com**, click on the 'Start Your Business' button. On the link for Chapter Three you will find a video interview with a former bank manager.

Key points

→ Research alone won't make a business successful. You have to exploit the potential you discover.

→ Market trends can be more significant than market size. It's the potential, not the past, that's important.

→ Banks and other lenders need reassurance that you know what you're doing as well as where you're going.

Next steps

What action will you take to apply the information in this chapter? By
when will you do it?

_____

_____

_____

_____

Business structure – building in room to grow

The most important thing to remember when structuring your new business is that it must be separate from your other affairs, especially where finances are concerned. Even if your enterprise is little more than a profitable hobby, it is still worthwhile keeping separate accounts and having a separate bank account. Let's consider how you can choose to structure your business.

Good order is the foundation of all things.

EDMUND BURKE

The three main business structures

There are essentially only three structures a business can have. These are:

→ sole trader – where you operate as a self-employed person;

→ partnership – two or more self-employed people working together;

→ limited company – a separate legal entity you own that employs yourself and possibly others.

Choosing the right structure is not straightforward. Much depends on you, your aspirations and your attitude to things such as risk and taxation.

Danger!

You want to get the right structure from the start. Most accountants will give you a free initial consultation. This is because they want to recruit you as a client. Use this opportunity to discuss your plans with a professional adviser.

Sole trader

This is the term used to describe a self-employed person. You have to account for your income and business expenses on your annual tax return and pay tax on your profits twice a year. It is advisable to keep your business transactions separate from your personal transactions.

If you have regular customers, you (and they) need to make sure that the tax authorities can't mistake you for an employee. It is important that you can be seen to be:

→ working for more than one customer;

→ clearly in control of what you do and when and how you do it;

→ providing your own tools and equipment;

→ able to subcontract or hire your own staff to do the work;

→ responsible for correcting any mistakes you make.

This can be a particular issue if you leave an organisation's employment and continue to work for them in a freelance capacity. It is an excellent way to secure your first client and some valuable income when you become self-employed, but you must make sure that you can be seen to be autonomous.

The pros:

→ Book-keeping is relatively simple.

→ You pay your tax twice a year.

→ Business-related costs and expenses can be set against tax.

The cons:

→ You might need to incorporate (set up a limited company) later.

→ You can be held personally liable for any debts.

→ Some organisations prefer to deal with a limited company.

A partnership

This essentially is two or more self-employed people working together. You can have differing shares in the partnership and pay tax on your share of the partnership profits. Partners can sell their share and new partners can buy in. It's a flexible structure. It is also possible to create a 'limited liability partnership' that gives each partner, as the name suggests, limited liability in the event of the partnership going bust or being sued.

Partnerships are:

→ the structure usually adopted by professional practices;

→ popular with husbands and wives who work together.

The pros:

→ Book-keeping remains relatively simple.

→ You can recruit an investor who is not active in the business (a sleeping partner).

→ Business-related costs and expenses can be set against tax.

The cons:

→ You can be held 'jointly and separately liable' for debts (in other words, if one partner defaults the others have to pay their share).

→ The partnership must be dissolved if a partner dies or becomes bankrupt.

→ You need a lawyer to help you put together a partnership agreement.

A limited company

This is a separate and distinct legal entity. It brings both benefits and restrictions. A limited company is the structure to go for if you:

→ plan to build a significant business;

→ want to raise money from investors;

→ expect to sell your business one day.

The pros:

→ You can issue and sell shares to raise investment.

→ The business is easier to sell (in part or entirely).

→ Your personal liability (as a director) is limited.

The cons:

→ Book-keeping is more complex and your accountancy bills higher.

→ Lenders and some suppliers will probably demand a persona guarantee, negating the benefits of limited liability.

→ There are higher costs associated with setting it up.

Toolkit

The Business Link website provides a useful guide to choosing the right structure for your business. Available at **http://www.businesslink.gov.uk/ bdotg/action/layer?r.l1=1073858805&topicId=1073865730&r.lc=en&r.l2 =1073859131&r.s=tl** or at **http://tinyurl.com/6h2az6**.

Time saver

Encourage your old boss to become one of your first customers. You'd be surprised how often they welcome the chance to retain some of your expertise.

Case study

James Bowles, Bowles Print Management UK, www.bpm-uk.co.uk

James Bowles was the Midlands sales manager for a Sussex printer with a good local customer base. When his employer went bust he decided to realise an ambition and start his own business.

He had customers and knew the print world. It was not difficult to find suppliers and set himself up as a print broker. He uses his buying power and expertise to provide his clients with excellent service at competitive prices. James makes a modest margin on each transaction.

'I am content with being a sole trader at the moment,' James told me. 'I have low overheads and business is tightly controlled within budgets. Accounting is also simple. Eventually, as we grow, we will become a limited company, but not yet.'

Why is it important to get this right?

Setting up your business is a clear signal to everyone that you are serious. This is not just an idea or dream, but something you're actually going to do. Choosing the right structure forces you to think about your longer-term goals. Will you be seeking investors? Will you work alone or with others? Are you hoping to sell your business one day?

It can also be very complicated to change the structure of a business once it's up and running. You really do need to take advice and get this right first time.

The person you are most likely to ask is an accountant.

Time saver

Take advice and get the right business structure from the start. It's far easier than changing things later.

How to choose an accountant

An accountant is in business to make money. They will have worked out the type of client they work best with and will hopefully set out their stall to attract the kind of business they want.

Accountants charge for their time by the hour, although many will negotiate an annual fee and allow you to pay this in monthly instalments.

When searching for an accountant, look for:

→ someone you can trust and relate to;

→ a firm with clients like you;

→ expertise in your type of business;

→ enthusiasm to welcome you as a new client.

Most accountants win new clients by introduction. Ask people whose opinion you respect to recommend a firm to you. Ask them to explain why they are happy to introduce them to you.

Other business structures

There are actually more than three possible structures you can adopt, although the three already mentioned are by far the most common. This is why it really is so important to take advice. This is particularly true if you are setting up a charity or social enterprise. There are specialist legal structures designed to meet the specific needs of both.

How to set up your business, step by step

Let's assume you have a name for your business (there are tips on choosing a name in Chapter Twelve). You have also decided what structure to go for, having hopefully taken some good advice from an accountant or other business adviser. Now you need to set up the business. Where do you start?

Step 1: banking

A good first step is to open a business bank account. This is vital as you must keep your business and personal banking separate. It is also really exciting to see your new chequebook and paying in book. It brings what has so far been a vision into reality.

When choosing your business bank, think about the following:

→ Using a different bank from the one you bank with personally. They might not be the best for your business and many entrepreneurs prefer to keep their personal finances totally separate.

→ Branch location, as you'll have to pay in cheques and possibly cash.

→ The quality of their online banking offer.

→ The account manager who'll be looking after you – will you get on?

Banks are different. You need to choose one that fits with your business aspiration. They fall into four broad categories:

→ **Simple.** These banks specialise in offering great value to businesses that require no more than a simple banking service. If you keep your account in credit, make only a modest number of transactions and don't want to borrow (much), they are perfect.

→ **Standard.** These are the main high street banks. They'll offer you an enticing array of incentives to open a business account and you'll have an account manager you can talk to. Most people start with one of these. As your business grows, they will be able to deal with your changing needs.

→ **Boutique.** There are a growing number of boutique banks. These are often non-British and pride themselves on their ability to configure tailor-made banking arrangements for people with non-standard needs. They are often the best bet if you are already wealthy or need to structure your personal and business debt in a particular way.

→ **Faith.** There are also a number of specialist banks that structure their banking services to comply with your faith or moral stance. The Islamic Bank of Britain, for example, provides Sharia-compliant banking that enables Muslim entrepreneurs to do business free of conflict with their religious beliefs. There are also banks that have more 'ethical' investment policies than others, as well as banks that specialise in social enterprises.

Whichever bank you choose, they will ask you for various facts, figures and documents, particularly if you're setting up a limited company. This gives you a useful checklist to work from.

Step 2: paperwork

The paperwork you need depends on the business structure you're setting up. As you might expect, the more complicated the structure, the more paperwork you'll need:

→ **Sole trader.** The only paperwork you need to become a sole trader is your chequebook, paying in book and ideally some business cards or fliers. It really can be as simple as that.

→ **Partnership.** You need no more paperwork to form a partnership than you do to start up as a sole trader. However, you would be well advised to pay a solicitor to draw up a simple partnership agreement. This defines what happens if your circumstances change. Even life

How to Start Your Own Business for Entrepreneurs

partners who start a business together often choose to have a formal partnership agreement. If nothing else, it helps you both to see the business as something separate from your relationship.

Time saver

Always have a simple, legal partnership agreement, even if your business partner is your best friend. It will avoid argument or time-consuming negotiations later on.

→ **Limited company.** A limited company is a separate legal entity and needs some legal documents to define its existence. Your bank will need to see these before opening your account. It will also require you to pass some company resolutions, but it will give you simple forms to fill in and sign to cover these.

Additional considerations for a limited company

Limited companies have to be registered (in the UK at Companies House). They also need to have a 'memo and arts' (short for Memorandum and Articles of Association). These are two legal documents that define the way the company is set up and the parameters within which it will operate.

There are a number of ways to set up a limited company, including the following:

→ **Specialist registration agents.** You see their adverts in business classifieds, offering a 'limited company for £50' and so on. These can be good value, but you need to be sure the standard 'memo and arts' they use does not restrict you. It costs money to change these documents.

→ **Your accountant.** This will cost more but probably work out cheaper in the long run. Your accountant will make sure the paperwork covers your specific needs. They will also register themselves with the tax authorities as your agent. This means they automatically get copies of all tax correspondence – one less thing for you to worry about.

→ **Yourself.** It is possible to do all this yourself direct with Companies House. However, your time can probably be better spent elsewhere.

You will also need to look at insurance. This is covered in Chapter Twenty-two.

Step 3: tax authorities

You are currently paying tax on your income, or have done so recently. You need to tell your tax office (or have your accountant tell them) that your situation has changed. If you are setting up a limited company, you will be employed by it. Otherwise you'll be effectively self-employed. You will have to complete an annual personal tax return or delegate this to your accountant.

You will also need to tell your local authority if you are occupying business premises so that you can pay business rates.

Finally, you will need to register for value-added tax if you expect your turnover to exceed the annual threshold. There are two key points to note about VAT:

→ You can voluntarily register if your turnover is below the threshold. This enables you to reclaim the tax paid on purchases, but you must also charge the tax on your sales.

→ You can reclaim the VAT on some of your set-up costs, such as computers, equipment and so on, when you make your first VAT return, even if you were not registered for VAT when the purchases were made. (There is a time limit for this; for the latest regulations, check **www.hmrc.gov.uk**.)

Time saver

If you sell to the general public, who cannot reclaim the VAT you charge, it might be more profitable for you to keep your annual sales below the threshold for VAT registration. This can give you a competitive advantage over larger, VAT-registered rivals and reduce the time spent on paperwork.

In some countries you will also need to register with your local Chamber of Commerce. In the UK membership is voluntary. This is not the case everywhere.

Case study
Keith Nicol, Costa Blanca TV, **www.CostaBlancaTV.com**

Keith Nicol has travelled the world as a professional film-maker and has also presented TV programmes. He married a Spanish woman and now lives in Spain with his wife and son. He makes his living making wedding and corporate videos.

Costa Blanca TV is very much Keith's brainchild. It's a web TV channel that will provide local news and views to the expat community in his area. Once established on the Costa Blanca, Keith plans to grow the business by franchising.

'At the moment, my business is virtual with my time being the biggest investment,' he explained. 'Once we are established and start to grow, I'll register as a company so that we are protected from some of the financial risk.'

Managing your company's finances is one of the more complex aspects of being an entrepreneur. For a more detailed guide to the entire process, see *Book-keeping and Accounts for Entrepreneurs*, another title in this series.

Frequently asked questions

Here are some typical questions asked by new entrepreneurs about the financial aspects of starting their business.

We're worried about bad debts and think that we should set up a limited company to protect ourselves. Do you agree?

There's no doubt that many people have come unstuck because of bad debt. However, rather than structure your business solely to protect you from the worst eventuality, set it up in a way that suits a more positive future. Then take all precautions to make sure you don't incur bad debts – for example, by taking customer deposits with orders to reduce your exposure.

My brother-in-law works for a firm of accountants and has offered to do our books, etc. for free. Is this a good idea?

Although it might cost you more, it is always good practice to keep some distance between your business and home lives. If you'd like to use your brother-in-law's services, do it via his firm so that the relationship remains professional.

My business will involve a lot of transactions in other countries. Should I go for a bank with a large overseas network?

I'd not make any assumptions that a large overseas network will make it easier for you to do foreign transactions. Meet the export advisers at a couple of banks and also talk to your local chamber of commerce. Then make your decision.

Another key decision you will face is finding the perfect business premises. The next chapter will address this.

Key points

→ You want to get the business structure right from the beginning; it can be costly to change.

→ Don't hire the cheapest professional advisers. Use people who will become increasingly valuable to you as your enterprise grows.

→ Choose the structure that best suits your needs and future aspiration. Don't incorporate just to save a little tax. Focus on making money, not saving tax!

Next steps

What action will you take to apply the information in this chapter? By when will you do it?

_____

_____

_____

_____

Finding the perfect place – business premises

Chapter Five

A surprising number of people run their business from home. It is certainly convenient and low cost when compared with the alternatives. In fact, many businesses are started at home and remain based there for many years. There is no shame in operating a home-based business.

For many there is no choice. They simply can't afford to rent or buy business premises. For others who can afford the choice, the decision might be more difficult. The short answer to the location conundrum is that you need to be where your customers need you to be.

 A desk is a dangerous place from which to watch the world. JOHN LE CARRÉ

Working from home: pros and cons

The economic benefits of working from home are obvious. You're not incurring any additional costs for rent or travel. Working in the back bedroom is very handy, particularly if you want to work odd hours to fit around childcare, for example.

Working from home is good if:

→ your customers do not expect to visit your place of work;

→ you have room to set aside for a dedicated office;

→ your business will not annoy or disturb your neighbours.

"I **am** working. Oprah is a great role model for entrepreneurs. Plus, I now know how to make a delicious macaroni salad."

Working from home is bad if:

→ your business will grow quickly and cause a nuisance;
→ you need to employ people and don't want them in your house;
→ you lack the self-discipline to ignore the TV/household chores/ garden and get on with the job.

Sir Richard Branson has always run his business from home. Although he now has a business empire, his core senior team work around him in what was until a few years ago the family home. To make more space, he bought and moved his family into the house next door.

Remember that the President of the USA and the Prime Minister of Great Britain both work from home!

How to work from home

If you're going to work from home, you need to make things as easy as possible for yourself and those you live with. A separate workspace is important, if only so you can focus when at work and forget when you're trying to relax. There are a number of things you can do to achieve this.

→ Invest in a dedicated business phone line, so you know whether you're being called by a customer or your mother. This also means you can opt not to take work calls in the evening without ignoring personal calls.
→ Buy yourself a decent desk and chair. You'll feel more professional if you avoid working at the dining room table.
→ Be disciplined about your time. Be either at work or at home. Don't let your multi-tasking bridge the gap.
→ If your clients do come to you at home (for instance, if you're a music teacher or therapist), keep tidy the parts of your home your visitors will use. Keep any clutter out of sight.
→ If you actually work from home, rather than at home, consider having your phone diverted to an answering service when you are out. Alternatively, make your mobile your work number and

emphasise the fact that this gives your customers rapid access to you. This compensates for the less professional image a mobile number may create.

Case study
Alison Pitman, The Phone Voice,
www.thephonevoice.com

Alison Pitman has always worked in broadcast journalism and was taught how to read news bulletins and make voice news reports. She saw requests for voiceover presenters on a marketplace website and realised this was something she could easily do from home. With a two-year-old daughter this was vital.

The technology she needed to record voiceovers was just affordable and she was soon in business.

'I never meet my customers as the majority are based overseas,' she explained. 'All my client interactions take place online via email, which is convenient for everyone. They email me a script, I record it and then email back the audio file. I could not combine work and childcare any other way.'

How to make space at home to work

Before discounting the idea of working from home on grounds of space alone, consider the cost/merits of:

→ converting your garage or loft;
→ buying a 'home office building' (which is effectively an insulated garden cabin, purpose built for year-round work use);

→ buying and adapting a used mobile home which, providing you treat it as an 'extension' to your home, may not need planning consent.

Web bonus

At our website, **www.forentrepreneursbooks.com,** click on the 'Start Your Business' button. On the link for Chapter Five you will find an extract from my book *The Entrepreneur's Book of Checklists*, entitled '10 Good Reasons to Work from Home'.

Alternatives to working from home

If working from home is not for you, there are plenty of alternatives. Some of them are obvious, such as renting space in a business centre. Others are less obvious but should not be overlooked. Less obvious alternatives include the following:

→ Working at one of your customers' premises. This clearly commits them to you and may actually create opportunities as well as save costs. Graphic design firms, virtual personal assistants, transport operators and book-keepers are all examples where this can function well.

→ Operating within a separate business. This can work well if your products or services complement those of your host. For example, a bag shop could be located within a ladies' fashion store or a café in an office complex.

→ A mobile business, where you take yourself and all your equipment in a van. This can work for carpet retailers, who take samples to the customer's home rather than trying to attract them to a shop.

Case study
Silvano Milano, Park 'n' Trim

Silvano Milano was a gents' barber who wanted the freedom of working for himself. He tried renting a chair in a barber's shop in town but became restless.

He preferred straightforward haircuts to elaborate styling and found he was losing out to more flamboyant rivals.

Then he had an idea. He bought a van and kitted it out as a barber's shop. He worked out a round that meant he spent half a day a week at ten different truck stops in his area. His theory was that truck drivers would welcome the chance to have a haircut during their compulsory rest breaks from driving. He was right and soon had a thriving business.

Finding premises

Sometimes it is simply not possible to start your business at home. It also might not be desirable. The premises you find for your new enterprise have to be affordable and add value to the enterprise.

There are a number of factors you need to consider when choosing business premises. The importance of each will vary, depending on what type of business you have, but all are significant.

Location

Where you site your business is important. This seems obvious, but you need to consider the following questions:

→ Will customers visit you and what impression will your location create?

→ How convenient is the location for you and any (future) employees?

→ Do you need to be near competitors? (Important in retail.)

→ Are you close to suppliers or others it may be useful to have around?

→ Is the place bright and inspiring or dismal and depressing?

→ Remember, too, that you're going to spend a lot of time at your new place of work. It has to be somewhere you're going to like being.

Tenure

When you start a business you're never totally sure what space you need. Retail is perhaps the only area where you have to commit to a place and stay there for some time, although even then, it's not unusual for shops to move to a more favourable location when the opportunity arises.

The key point here is to give yourself as much flexibility as possible. Think about the following:

→ How long is the lease? Short leases can be cheap, but you'll have to move somewhere else at the end – perfect if you're anticipating rapid growth!

→ What breaks are there in the lease? These are the points at which you can move out without financial penalty. Note that if you sign a year-long lease, you are committed to paying a year's rent, even if you move out early.

→ Security of tenure. Be aware that most business tenancies are written in such a way that you do not have the same security of tenure as you would with a residential lease. Remember that breaks in leases work both ways. Your landlord can also ask you to move out if they need the space themselves.

→ Maintenance and repairs. You will inevitably be responsible for some of these costs. Be sure you understand what they are from the start

In other words

A **tenancy** is the right to occupy land or buildings as provided by the terms of a lease or other agreement. A lease is the legal agreement by which you occupy that land or buildings.

Time saver

Take legal advice before signing a lease to avoid surprise repair bills or lengthy negotiations later.

Rent

Unless you can afford to buy premises, you need to pay rent. Most business landlords ask for rent monthly or quarterly in advance. Some will ask for a deposit as well. When working out how much your premises will cost, bear in mind the following:

→ VAT. Some landlords charge VAT on top of the rent and some don't. If you're not planning to register for VAT you won't be able to reclaim it.

→ Rates. In the UK, you will need to pay business rates to the local council on top of your rent. This is calculated on the 'rateable value' of the premises. Some councils subsidise the rates charge for smaller business premises, specifically to help small businesses.

→ Extras. Your rent may or may not include heat and light, broadband, parking and cleaning.

Retail premises

If you are in retail, you need to consider some additional points when choosing a location. These include the following:

→ Do you want to be close to competitors or not? This can be good for restaurants as people often browse menus outside before making their choice. It can be bad if you're a laundrette, where you want to be the only place in the neighbourhood.

→ What do the neighbours do? A tattoo parlour may not prosper in a shopping centre and a chocolatier may not do well in the arty bohemian quarter of the city.

→ Who shops in the locality? What is the demographic profile of the local population? Can they afford what you're going to sell?

→ Footfall. The more you can attract passing trade, the less you will need to advertise to attract people through the door.

How to Start Your Own Business for Entrepreneurs

Researching retail locations

There is so much theory about how to find your perfect retail location that it's easy to get confused. Big retailers conduct detailed street surveys, look at demographic data for a shopping centre's catchment area and count how many people walk along the street.

It is true to say that the more the right kind of people walk past the door, the more of them will be drawn in. It's equally correct to say that you can pay too much for a location that delivers many passing customers.

Shop rents are largely dictated by location and footfall. Rent too good a location and you won't necessarily see sufficient additional turnover to cover the additional cost.

One of the best ways to research retail locations is to visit them. This sounds obvious, but time spent sitting in a coffee shop watching people walking along a street that you are considering can be time well spent. Your instinct will usually tell you as much as the shop landlord's promotional material.

Time saver

Start your location research by loitering and looking. Seeing is believing!

Top property tips

Before committing yourself to workspace, be sure to think about the following:

→ It is possible to rent a desk as well as an office. You can often find these advertised online.

→ Consider sharing premises. If you work mainly for one customer, perhaps making components, it might be possible to base yourself on their site. You might also set up a 'shop within a shop' – for example, a conservatory showroom at a garden centre.

→ Never be afraid to negotiate. Your landlord probably needs you more than you need them.

Frequently asked questions

Finding the right place to work is important. Here are some typical concerns.

Working from home makes sense for my new business, but how can I avoid the temptation to spend the whole day in my pyjamas?
You need to be disciplined in having fixed working hours and a separate place to work, and for some people it helps to dress for work as well, even if they are spending the day alone in the home office.

I have the opportunity to base my company at one of my clients' premises. However, I am worried that other clients might be put off if I am based within another company.
Basing yourself within a customer's premises means that you are pretty much assured of getting their business. Add to this the benefit of lower overheads and you can see why it can be a good idea. You need to invest some of that cost saving in making sure that you are seen as an independent business and not simply a department within your customer's company. For example, you need a separate telephone line, some signage that announces your presence and ideally your own front door.

A good friend has offered us the opportunity to set up our shop within their shop. This means we can sell to their customers, and as our customer base grows our customers will also buy from our friend. Our product ranges fit well together. The problem is that our friend is reluctant to put anything in writing – should we be worried about this?
I am sure your friend is offering to help you for all the right reasons. However, entering into any sort of business arrangement with a friend, or for that matter with family, is fraught with danger. When things aren't going well, everything will be fine, but if one or other of you starts to do significantly better than the other, tension can rise. For your peace of mind, you need some kind of written agreement, ideally prepared by a solicitor. Then you both know exactly what you are committing to do.

One alternative you may not have considered is taking over an existing business instead of starting from scratch. In the next chapter we'll look at the benefits and drawbacks of doing this.

Key points

→ Working from home can be great and is not second best.

→ You need to retain the flexibility to move premises as your business grows.

→ Don't be afraid to question the terms of a lease or to ask for the things you want included to be included.

→ Think very carefully before you sell the family home to buy a business that has accommodation, such as a pub. Better to rent a pub until you are totally confident it is the right business for you.

Next steps

What action will you take to apply the information in this chapter? By when will you do it?

_____   _____

_____

_____   _____

_____

Starting up or taking over an existing enterprise

You might think it strange that a book about starting a business should suggest that you might take one over instead. The reality is, though, that sometimes taking over an existing business will be a better option.

You might also think that buying an existing business is beyond your reach. However, sometimes it costs less to take over an existing business than to start from scratch.

> **It is our choices ... that show what we truly are, far more than our abilities.** J. K. ROWLING

Case study
Howard Schultz, Starbucks, www.starbucks.co.uk

When Howard Schultz joined Starbucks in the early 1980s, the company was already a highly respected local roaster and retailer of whole bean and ground coffees. A business trip to Italy opened his eyes to the rich tradition of the espresso beverage. Espresso drinks became an essential element of Schultz's vision. He purchased Starbucks with the support of local investors in 1987.

Since then he has grown a business, which was unknown outside Seattle, into a global brand, with more than 6,000 coffee shops in 30 countries. The success of Howard Schultz clearly demonstrates how much better it can be to buy an established business and grow it than to start from scratch.

Why take over an existing business?

The value of an existing business lies mostly within its:

→ customer base – specifically the likelihood that these customers will continue to buy;

→ reputation – which will encourage the customer base to grow;

→ potential – the market trends that mean future growth is likely;

→ intellectual property – essentially the exclusivity the business has to exploit knowledge and inventions;

→ balance sheet – the things the business owns that will be included in the sale, including debtors.

If you are eager and enthusiastic, or perhaps bring with you a customer base or marketplace reputation, you might need an established infrastructure to support you.

Why do people sell their business?

To understand why you might be able to afford to buy a business you need to understand why people decide to sell. The motivation for selling will influence both the price and the time period over which you will have to pay. Buying a business is not as simple as buying a house or car.

People sell their business for one or more of a number of reasons. For example:

→ they want to retire or no longer have the good health to continue;

→ they're getting divorced and own the business with their ex;

→ they've lost interest or perhaps even lost the plot;

→ bad debts or management mistakes mean they have no cash;

→ the business has outgrown their ability to manage it effectively.

The skill of buying a business is to work out the vendor's motivation and match your offer to both of your needs.

Time saver

Sometimes it can be good simply to buy into a business rather than buy it outright. This means you retain the vendor's interest and participation. It also means you can buy the business a little at a time.

When is it better to start from scratch?

However appealing the idea of buying an existing business may seem, there are times when you'll be better to start from scratch. There are lots of benefits to creating a business from nothing. These include:

- → a marketplace with no preconceived ideas or expectations;
- → the opportunity to be new, fresh and different from competitors;
- → an ability to set your own pace, perhaps starting part-time.

However, don't fall for the myth that you will be starting a unique business. No business is truly unique. People need to compare your enterprise with others before they will see and understand the value you bring. Their innate suspicion of the unknown will make it difficult to market something really revolutionary and new.

Case study
Julie Begbie, Keepstakes, **www.keepstakes.co.uk**

When Julie Begbie was on maternity leave with her second child, she started looking for business ideas. She wanted to work flexibly so that she could do the school run and be around when her children needed her. Julie also wanted a business she could be passionate about. She wanted to enjoy what she did as well as succeed.

She knew she liked making things, and when a friend's baby received a tree with a handmade plaque, inspiration struck. The plan that led to the launch of Keepstakes grew and the business was born. Keepstakes makes personalised plaques that create unique, lasting gifts and keepsakes.

Julie did not rush into the business from day one. She chose instead to grow it slowly and steadily. When the time came that income from the business was enough to justify resigning from her job, she took the plunge and hasn't looked back since. Buying a business wasn't an option for Julie. She wanted to combine creating her business with the needs of her young children.

What do you want?

Before looking to see whether a business is for sale, you have to work out what you're looking to buy. If you have a specific skill or interest, you need to focus there. If, on the other hand, your background is in general management, you want to keep a relatively open mind. Look for business models you understand, not just industry sectors where you have experience.

How to find a business for sale

Many businesses are advertised as being for sale, through classified advertising in magazines such as *Dalton's Weekly*, on specialist websites and through specialist brokers called 'business transfer agents'. Other places to look include:

→ accountants, who will often discreetly market a client's business;

→ your employer, who might be receptive to you buying out all or a part of their organisation;

→ people within your existing business network who might know someone who's thinking of selling.

You don't have to be in business to join a business network. Become active in forums where you might meet or hear about the right business opportunity. There's nothing wrong with going to networking events as someone 'looking to buy into the industry'. You want to be noticed by people who might approach you.

Time saver

The more people you tell that you are looking for a business, the quicker you are likely to find opportunities.

Make an offer

Often the best way to buy a business is to find one you think may meet your needs and suggest a buyout to the owner. It can be very flattering to receive an approach from a prospective buyer, so don't worry about upsetting the owner. It's rather like receiving a call from a headhunter at work; you may be happy in your job, but it's nice to be offered an alternative.

Signs to look out for include the following:

→ **Complacency**. This is best illustrated in the retail sector, but it is equally true of all business types. The shop owner that has become complacent might:
— not keep window displays up to date;
— be slow to repair damage, such as broken lights;
— have demotivated staff;
— carry old, dusty stock;
— be slow to serve you and be unenthusiastic.

→ **Not keeping up**. This often means that any competitive advantage is eroded as interest may be waning. Signs that a business is slipping behind can include:
— lack of recent investment in vehicles and technology;
— slow response to changing market trends;
— lapsed membership of trade and business networks;
— reduction in marketing expenditure.

→ **Running out of money**. This is indicated by:
— County Court judgments;
— redundancies;
— suppliers beginning to talk/rumour.

→ **Personal problems**. Divorce is not the only personal problem that can mean a business owner might be willing to sell. Others include:
— illness or death of a partner/shareholder;
— boardroom arguments/partner disagreements;
— prosecution for a serious offence;
— an ambition to do something new.

How to buy a business, step by step

You cannot buy a business without professional help. Your accountant and solicitor are crucial in making sure you don't make a big mistake. They will inevitably lack your enthusiasm for the deal you're trying to do. They will also encourage you to explore aspects of the purchase that you might otherwise overlook.

What you need to remember is that professional advisers have dealt with many similar transactions. You will be emotionally involved and have bought the dream. They simply look at the stark facts and guide you through the following steps.

Valuing a business

Working out what a business is worth is not as straightforward as valuing a house. This is because there is much more to consider than simply the asset value of the enterprise. Value is largely dependent on the enterprise's future potential to generate profit.

A major part of that future potential will depend on your ability to manage the business. If you know the sector, are well connected and have the skills to build up what you are buying, the value to you is greater than if you do not. Large organisations often buy (and sell) a business to improve their distribution or to align themselves with a wider corporate vision. This can also distort a business's value.

Most people selling a business will make the running and suggest a price. You and your advisers need to explore:

→ assets such as premises, plant and equipment;
→ past trading performance;
→ future trading projections;
→ customer 'stickiness' (volume of repeat business);
→ current accounts (debtors, creditors, work in progress);
→ any patents or trade agreements that maintain exclusivity;
→ motivation for selling (the more the vendor wants to sell, the better your bargaining position).

You also need to be confident that you fully appreciate what's happening in the business's marketplace – for example:

→ Is demand growing or waning?
→ Is market share increasing or decreasing? (If the market is growing at 10 per cent per annum and the business is growing at 5 per cent per annum, it is actually losing market share.)

- → Are competitors gaining ground?
- → What impact will planned or predicted legislation have?
- → What innovation is there within the business and within the market-place?

Danger!

Ignore your instinct at your peril. However good something looks, only proceed if it feels right.

Danger

Doing the deal

Contrary to what you might believe, few businesses actually sell for the asking price in one cash sum. That's because savvy buyers negotiate a deal that enables them to spread their risk and, as far as possible, lets the business they're buying generate the money needed to pay off the former owner. Typical types of company transaction include:

- → earn out – where the vendor remains with the business and the money they actually get is linked directly to trading performance;
- → earn in – where you pay an agreed price from your share of the profits generated (this is how new partners often acquire a share of their firm);
- → various performance-related deals – where the vendor leaves but is paid sums that are linked to company performance over a period of years;
- → staged purchase – where you might buy a trading company and have an agreed deal to buy the premises it occupies later.

The vendor will want to minimise their tax liability on the sale proceeds. There can be a financial incentive for them to sell the business in stages over a number of years.

Due diligence

This is where your advisers (usually your accountant and solicitor) really earn their fees. As well as helping you to structure and perhaps negotiate the deal, they will look at:

How to Start Your Own Business for Entrepreneurs

- → the management accounts, to determine true profitability (many owner-managers take income from the business in several ways and so the business might be more profitable than it appears at first glance);
- → contracts with customers and suppliers, to find problems and liabilities;
- → employee contracts, staff rights and liabilities that might transfer to you – for example, pension rights and profit-sharing schemes;
- → any current legal disputes that might impact on the deal;
- → environmental commitments and risk;
- → infrastructure issues, such as IT systems.

The most important element of all to bear in mind when buying a business is to be totally confident that you can make it work. It is almost always better to walk away from a deal you don't feel comfortable with than to risk burdening yourself with a business that will cause you problems. This is quite different from starting up from scratch, where you should be encouraged to talk to prospective customers and experiment, rather than spend too much time trying to work out what's going to succeed for you.

Frequently asked questions

The following are some of the types of questions asked about taking over a business.

I've been talking with the family of a garage owner who is now in prison for growing cannabis at his business premises. Do you think the owner's chequered history will harm my chances of rebuilding the business if I buy it?
There's no doubt that reputation can work both ways. That said, if the owner is in prison, he's not going to get as good a price for the garage as he would if he'd not suddenly abandoned it when arrested. Drive a hard bargain, with compassion, and don't try to conceal the reason for the takeover. Notoriety can be a selling point.

There's a derelict shop in my market town that I think would make a wonderful café. It's just come on to the market. It's a wreck but would be stunning if restored sensitively. What do you think?

Which do you want to do most? Open a cafe or restore an old building? Both can be profitable if tackled separately. Both can fail if tackled together. Only embark on this kind of project if you have more money than you think you'll need. For one thing, the restoration might well go over budget, and for another, your café might not open as soon as you might hope.

I'm negotiating to take over a flagging print business. The owner is past retiring age and is losing customers, but he won't accept anything like a realistic price. How can I encourage him to see sense?
You probably can't. He's worked on his own for maybe 30 years and may never have taken advice from anyone. Walk away but stay friends. Keep your eye on things because, almost inevitably, the decline will continue. If you do end up getting a deal some time in the future, be kind to him. Don't say, 'If we'd done this ages ago you'd have got a better price.'

Key points

→ Don't assume that you have to start a business from scratch. Sometimes you can buy something that's up and running.

→ If you want to buy a business, spread the word. It might encourage someone to surprise you!

→ Remember that your business might also have a greater value to someone else than to yourself. Be receptive to offers, even if you decide not to accept them.

Next steps

What action will you take to apply the information in this chapter? By when will you do it?

_____

_____

_____

_____

Planning to succeed

Part Two

How to write a convincing plan

The business adage, 'If you fail to plan you are planning to fail,' is perhaps one of the truest pieces of advice anyone can give you. But that does not mean a business plan has to be a large or complex document. Nobody measures a business plan by its length. Keep it short and to the point.

The best business plan is the one you write yourself that is short, is simple to understand and, above all else, believably illustrates how you plan to realise a personal vision.

Although others would advise that your business plan should be written to appeal to your bank manager, it is actually more important that the document means a lot to you. Bank managers have a habit of spotting when a plan has been written purely to encourage them to lend money.

They will learn all they need about you, your business ambition and ability in the first ten minutes of conversation with you. The most ambitious, complicated, cleverly written business plan in the world will not sway the bank manager whose first impression is that you haven't got what it takes to succeed.

Conversely, a concise, explicit plan that shows you have researched your idea, have thought about what you are going to do and understand the basic rules of business is more than enough, providing that you also are passionate, persuasive and convincing face to face.

 Life is what happens to you while you're busy making other plans. JOHN LENNON

What does a good business plan contain?

The best business plans are often the shortest. They summarise in two or three pages the opportunity, the challenges and the resources needed to make it happen. While the business plan is a serious document, there is nothing wrong with illustrating it with pictures and graphs. The objective is to communicate clearly and quickly.

The narrative is supported by a single-page spreadsheet that summarises cash flow for the first 12 months. This shows what money is needed to establish the business and ideally also charts the initial signs of profitability.

Even if you are not confident about writing a business plan yourself, it's a good idea to try, and then simply ask someone else to help work on it further. Your business plan has to be exactly that: *your* business plan. Only you know what you want to achieve, and you need to explore and express that in your own words. Once you have done this, you can ask someone to tidy the document up and correct any spelling and grammatical errors.

Of course, the plan also has to be appropriate to the scale of the business you are starting. If you are going to work from home as a tradesman or consultant, becoming effectively self-employed, you need a less detailed plan than if you are planning with your colleagues to buy out part of your employer's company.

However much detail your plan actually requires, it is always good practice to begin with a simple two-page summary. For some that will be all they need; for others it merely sets the scene for the detail that will follow.

Time saver

If you're starting a simple business, you only need a simple plan.

Case study

Jeff Clark, Admiral Printers, **www.admiralprinters.com**

When Jeff Clark reached 40, his wife told him it was time to plan the second half of his career. There were, she said, 20 years left to realise their ambition.

The couple decided to start a business together and began to look around. They wanted a business they could relate to, that met a clear market need. They also wanted a business that would allow them to build and maintain relationships with other businesspeople, rather than provide a one-off service.

Their research and their backgrounds led them to buy an existing printing company. New to print, they kept on the existing employees and set out to grow their new enterprise. Jeff's business plan acknowledged the fact that the print industry was in decline, but identified that, by introducing design, focusing on service and adding real value to each job, they could buck the downward industry trend.

After six years of trading, turnover has more than doubled and profits have grown.

Why a short business plan is better than a long plan

It is very tempting to write a traditional and comprehensive business plan, particularly if you are following one of the many templates provided by the banks and business support agencies.

Writing a short plan has several benefits. For example:

→ it will be easier to read and remember;

→ it will force you to be focused and specific;

→ busy people – for example, bank managers and business angels – will be able to make a rapid assessment and quickly spot the pertinent facts.

Remember that it can take longer to write a short business plan than a long one. That's because the process makes you think. Thinking is good!

Who needs to read your plan and why?

Your business plan should be your business route map, summarising the journey and identifying when you need to refuel and who you need to pick up along the way. A good business plan is one that you choose to keep close and handy, rather than filed away in a drawer.

Initially your business plan's function is convincing you and perhaps those close to you that the enterprise you are proposing will succeed. In fact, it is often a good idea to let your life partner critique your business plan before you release it for wider circulation. They won't necessarily understand the business you are about to begin, but they will understand you and challenge you if they think you are being unrealistic or too bold.

Other people who might need to see your business plan include the following:

→ **Bank manager.** Even if you are not planning to borrow money, the manager of your business bank account will want to see a business plan. You need to be enthusiastic about your enterprise. Encourage your bank manager to give critical feedback.

→ **Landlord.** Particularly if you are starting a retail business, it is important for the landlord to know that they are renting to a business that will become successful. If you were a landlord with a prime retail location to let, you would need convincing to let it to a new business rather than to a more established operator.

→ **Investor.** Business investors come in all shapes and sizes. One thing that unites them all is that they will want to see and question a credible business plan before parting with any money.

→ **Key employees.** Although most new UK businesses do not employ staff, some do. If you are recruiting a key person whose commitment is vital to your success, it makes sense for them to road, understand and believe in your business plan.

Time saver

List the key points of your business plan and pin them on the wall next to your desk. They'll help you keep on track.

How to write a business plan, step by step

Here are the essential components of a successful business plan and a suggested format for each, with examples.

Your vision

This is one paragraph that captures exactly what your business is going to achieve and why that is important.

> Example: *'Blue Sky Home Care will provide sensitive, flexible and responsible care services that enables older people to remain in their homes rather than move to residential care.'*

It is important that the vision statement promises clear benefits to the customer group as well as to you as the entrepreneur. Your business needs to meet a recognised need, as well as realising your ambition.

Why you?

Next, you need a paragraph that explains why you are uniquely placed to make this business work.

> Example: *'After five years of commissioning domiciliary care for older people in my job at the council, I know exactly what service commissioners, service users and their families expect. Having audited service suppliers for three of those years I also know what makes both the difference and a profit.'*

Outline why your recent experience, knowledge and network clearly demonstrate that you are the one person who can make this happen.

Market share

How big is the market you are aiming at, where is it and how much are you planning to take?

> Example: *'There are currently 60,000 elderly people receiving domiciliary care in my borough. Demographics suggest that this number will grow by 10 per cent a year over the next ten years. We plan to grow to deliver 10 per cent of that market within three years.'*

You do not need to quote detailed statistics or data to prove that you know your market. Many people make the mistake of duplicating pages of facts and figures. All you need are those that matter.

Products/services

Now explain exactly what you will be selling and to whom.

> Example: *'We will offer three levels of care: bronze, silver and gold. If the council are funding the bronze level, family will be encouraged to pay the difference to upgrade their aged relative. Silver and gold levels will include extra services such as ironing, shopping and cooking.'*

Profit

Show in summary how your selling price is calculated. A one-page spreadsheet projecting your first year's cash flow is also needed, detailing how your overhead costs will be covered and identifying any need for borrowing.

> Example: *'The attached spreadsheet shows how we have calculated that our services will be charged on an all-inclusive, weekly basis. Profitability will be higher on the silver and highest at the gold service level.'*

This information needs to be backed up with service prices, ideally compared with competitor pricing, to show where you will fit in your marketplace.

People

Describe briefly the skills you need and how you will recruit, develop and retain the best people for the job.

> Example: *'I am a qualified general manager. We will build our own bank of care and domestic workers on flexible contracts to meet operational needs. We have an arrangement with the local college to audit and develop our people's skills.'*

Will you subcontract, use agency staff or employ people? Show you've considered the risk as well as the opportunity.

Exit strategy

Although you might not see yourself selling the business in the foreseeable future, it's important to show that you've thought about what happens when you've had enough.

> Example: *'My daughter is training as a social worker and after gaining a few years' work experience, plans to join me in the business and then take over from me when I retire in ten years' time.'*

Time saver

Use hyperlinks to connect the key statistics you have found to the source material. It makes the plan easier to read and lets people explore the detail if they choose.

Frequently asked questions

The following are some typical questions that new entrepreneurs may ask about business plans after reading this book.

I need to borrow money to start my busines, and a consultant has suggested I would do better with a professionally written plan than one I had prepared myself. What do you think?
A slick business plan written for you may well impress a business angel or funder. The problems will arise when they start asking questions and expect you to know the answers. A business plan, however well written, cannot create a business without an entrepreneur. Your plan needs to fit you as much as it does your business.

You suggest that the vision statement for my business should explain how the business can help other people, but actually deep down all I really want to do is help myself. Is this really a problem?
Every business needs customers, and those customers need to see clearly that the value they are gaining by dealing with you is greater than the cost. You need to be convinced that this is what you are doing before you can convince them.

I have read this chapter and I know what you're suggesting but I am still finding it difficult to get started. Can you help?

It could be that your business idea is not yet fully formed in your mind. If that is the case, perhaps you need to do more research. If, on the other hand, the problem is simply a lack of inspiration, take a look around on the internet and see how other businesses describe themselves. If you look hard enough you will probably find some sample business plans you can download and use to get you started.

Web bonus

At our website, **www.forentrepreneursbooks.com**, click on the 'Start Your Business' button. On the link for Chapter Seven you will find a list of websites where you can download business plan templates.

Key points

→ The best business plans are short and to the point. Less can mean more.

→ Write the plan with the reader in mind.

→ Remember that the benefits to your customers have to be worth more than they will cost.

Next steps

What action will you take to apply the information in this chapter? By when will you do it?

_____

_____

_____

_____

Where to find the money you need

Chapter Eight

Every new business needs funding to some extent. Even if you are simply going to sell your time, work from home and use the family car to get to clients' premises, you will have a cash flow gap to fill.

It is unusual to be paid in advance for the work that you do, and if you supply businesses you may have to wait 30, 60 and often 90 days before receiving payment. While you are waiting to be paid, you still have your day-to-day living expenses to cover, the car to run, the mortgage to pay and probably some specific business expenses to find money for as well.

You also need to have some rainy day money put to one side for the inevitable month when things go wrong or sales are slow. Just as a financial adviser will encourage you to have three months' salary in the bank to act as a buffer, so as an entrepreneur you need room to manoeuvre, too.

It is a sobering fact to learn that the single biggest cause of business failure is running out of money. Conversely, keeping on top of cash flow and making sure you focus on the most profitable work you do is the biggest cause of business success.

A bank is a place that will lend you money if you can prove that you don't need it. BOB HOPE

Working out how much money you need

Calculating how much money you need to establish and grow your business for the first year or two is rather like guessing the length of that proverbial piece of string. There are so many variable factors to consider that it is easy to miscalculate. It is easy to fool yourself into thinking that you need less than you really do.

Danger!

Don't kid yourself when working out your business budget. It's better to err on the side of caution and overestimate rather than underestimate how much money you will need.

How to Start Your Own Business for Entrepreneurs

Here are some factors you will need to take into account when calculating how much money you need to start your business:

→ **Living expenses.** It may well be several months before your new business is able to pay you. You need to factor your living expenses for the first few months into your start-up cost calculations.

Toolkit

It can be harder than you think to work out how much money you need each month to cover your living expenses. There's a useful online calculator at **http://www.thisismoney.co.uk/household-budget-calculator** or at **http://tinyurl.com/cled7y**.

→ **Equipment.** Depending on the business you are starting, you will need to equip yourself. This may be as simple as buying a new computer or as involved as fitting out a shop or factory unit.

→ **Stock and materials.** If you are going to make or retail anything, you will need to carry stock and buy raw materials. For example, if you are opening a restaurant you may need to furnish and decorate it or fit or perhaps modernise the kitchen. You will also need to stock the larder and wine cellar. And don't forgot crockery, cutlery, glasses and table linen. Make a list of what you need and work out what it's going to cost.

→ **Marketing.** You will need to launch your new business and promote it to prospective customers. Even if you are going to promote your business purely by word of mouth, you will need a website and business stationery. Invite a couple of marketing companies to suggest a launch campaign and budget. You don't have to accept their offer but it's useful to know what marketing can cost. For a guide to creating your own one-year marketing plan, see *Marketing for Entrepreneurs*, one of the other titles in this series.

→ **Premises.** You will probably rent premises to start with and will find that many landlords look for several months' rent in advance. You may also have to pay legal fees to set up a lease. Even if you decide to work from home, you may have to make some alterations and will certainly need additional insurance. Again, make a list.

→ **Money.** Borrowing money costs money. In your calculations, allow for bank fees and charges incurred in setting up an overdraft or bank loan. Your bank will often ask to take a second charge over your home. This means they have your house as security should you default on repayments. You may have to pay a valuation fee as well. Bank fees are often added to the loan, but they need to be allowed for all the same.

Toolkit

The VAT you pay on the things you purchase to set up your business can be claimed back on your first VAT return, even if you have not registered for VAT when you start. There is a time limit for this. For details, check **www.hmrc.gov.uk**.

Why too much is better than too little

There is no such thing as having too much money to start a business. Money gives you choice and flexibility. Too little money and you will find yourself becoming anxious about cash flow. The one thing you need to minimise when you start a business is your anxiety!

When you produce your cash flow forecast you will make assumptions about when people will pay you. Picture a spreadsheet with each vertical column representing one month. The top half of the spreadsheet will show your income and the bottom half your expenditure. Usually that is the way these statements are prepared. The very top line shows the opening balance in the bank and the very bottom line the closing balance.

You don't need much imagination to appreciate that if your income is delayed by one month, you have two months' running costs to cover instead of just one. This could have a dramatic effect on your bank balance. In fact, it is just this effect that leads rapidly growing businesses to run out of money. It is the time gap between incurring costs and banking the revenue those costs generate. This is why managing cash flow is so important.

This table assumes people pay promptly, within one month:

Month	1	2	3	4
Opening balance	£1,000	£500	£1,000	£1,500
Sales income	£0	£1,000	£1,000	£1,000
Purchases	£500	£500	£500	£500
Closing balance	£500	£1,000	£1,500	£2,000

This table assumes people pay late, in three months:

Month	1	2	3	4
Opening balance	£1,000	£500	£0	£500
Sales income	£0	£0	£1,000	£1,000
Purchases	£500	£500	£500	£500
Closing balance	£500	£0	£500	£1,000

You can see that in the second table you find yourself with no money in the bank at the end of month two. This very simple example shows how a small shift in payment date can have a major impact on your cash flow.

Clearly one way round this is to pay your suppliers late as well. Unfortunately, suppliers are unlikely to give a new company credit and may even demand cash with order for the first few months. This widens the gap further.

Never be ashamed of the fact that you're starting a new business. Many people will understand how important cash flow is and, if asked, will pay their invoices in part or in full before they are due. This helps cash flow and enables you to build a cash buffer.

How to self-fund your new business

Even if interest rates are low, borrowing money can be expensive. Furthermore, most banks will look for personal guarantees and possibly want to take second charge over your property. This means that should your business fail, you will have to find the money to repay the bank.

It makes sense, therefore, to borrow as little as you can, as cheaply as you can. Whichever way you look at it, if you have borrowed from the bank you are the one taking the financial risk. Here are some ways you can fund your business yourself.

Increase the mortgage

By far the cheapest source of business finance is to increase the mortgage on your home. Clearly you should not do this without taking professional advice. Many business starters negotiate a flexible mortgage deal, which enables them to draw out money and repay it without incurring costly fees or penalties.

The business benefit of borrowing against the value of your home is that you can spread the repayment over several years. What's more, if you have a flexible mortgage, together with plenty of self-discipline, you can take a repayment holiday if necessary.

Ask customers to pay in advance

It is not unusual for a customer to agree to staged payments to help your cash flow. Customers have every incentive to see your business grow, as it widens their choice of supplier. In some cases customers may even be prepared to make significant pre-payments to get you started. This has the added benefit of guaranteeing their commitment to buy from you. Your bank, in particular, will be encouraged by this.

Ask suppliers to extend credit

Your suppliers will be keen to support you as a new customer. They may be willing to help by allowing you extended credit to ease your cash flow in the early months. It is always worth asking them this. However, if they do allow you to pay late, make sure you pay promptly. You do not want the concession withdrawn.

Gilbert's strategy for finding the money he needs may not be ideal.

Case study

Claire Zorlutuna, Made in Mummy,
www.madeinmummy.com

Pregnant with her second child, Claire Zorlutuna had become quite irritated that not one retailer seemed to stock a decent range of fashionable clothes for mums-to-be. Then she was made redundant from her sales job while on maternity leave and decided to set up an online business to provide just that.

She had help from Business Link to write a robust business plan and borrowed from the bank to set up her online shop. To keep borrowings as low as possible, she negotiated supplier deals that mean she doesn't have to carry stock. Overheads were kept low by working from home.

The website launched in early 2009 and is already proving a success.

Why do you need investors?

Even if you have the money to self-fund, it doesn't necessarily mean that you are the most appropriate person to invest. The earlier points about seeking working capital from customers and suppliers can often make more sense.

Most businesses need investment as they grow. This is because a growing business needs to spend money on people, products and premises before the revenue from those investments pay off.

There is an important distinction between bank funding and external investment. Bank lending tends to be short term, and overdrafts, in particular, can be called in at a moment's notice – as the small print inevitably states, .

Where to look for outside investors

Hermann Hauser, founder of Acorn Computers and now a business investor, says that the first places you should look for funding are 'family and fools'. This seemingly harsh statement is totally true. That's because any investor will need to believe in you first and your business proposition second. Your family and friends know you best, so they will naturally have faith in your ability to deliver.

Fools are another matter. While there are people around foolish enough to invest in almost anything, that is not what Hauser meant. More his point was that people who believe in you are likely to make what to the outsider can seem like a foolish investment.

Whoever you recruit to invest in your business, they will want a return on their investment. Even your mother will expect a payback – even if it's just the satisfaction of seeing you succeed.

There are more places to look for investment than it first appears. All will demand a good business plan and a strong pitch, but each will make different demands on you in terms of return on their investment.

Small Firms Loan Guarantee Scheme

Your local business support agency can help you to apply for a loan under this UK government scheme. It is designed for situations where a bank is happy to lend you the money, but there's not enough security to cover the loan. For example, you may want to borrow £10,000 but your partner (who jointly owns the family home) is not prepared to allow the bank to take a charge over it. The government guarantees the loan and what is in effect an insurance premium is added to the loan to cover the risk.

Good points:	Bad points:
Enables you to borrow when otherwise the banks would say no	Can be costly to set up, although charges are usually added to the loan
The lender does not take any shares in your business	Can take a long time to set up

Grants

Sometimes you can obtain a grant to help cover the cost of setting up your business. The availability of grant funding and the eligibility criteria to receive grants are constantly changing.

Grants are most often focused on funding:

→ business establishment in deprived communities or by people battling with disadvantage;

→ capital equipment needed to compete in a regionally strategic usiness sector;

→ training and development of you and those you employ;

→ environmental good practice;

→ social enterprise.

Government business advisers can advise you on grants. There are also a number of online databases you can search.

Toolkit

Start your online search at **www.grantfinder.co.uk** or at **www.j4b.co.uk.**

Good points:	Bad points:
Enable you to fund stuff you otherwise could not afford	The application process can be long and complicated
Grants do not have to be paid back	It can be tempting to do something because there's a grant available

Prince's Trust www.princes-trust.org.uk

Founded and led by HRH Prince Charles, this charity provides a range of support to disadvantaged young people (aged under 30).

For budding entrepreneurs, it provides:

→ free business advice and start-up training;

→ unsecured business loans at preferential rates;

→ small grants;

→ two years' free business mentoring by an established volunteer business mentor.

Good points:	Bad points:
Offers sound advice and practical support to those who need it most	It has a finite budget and can't support as many as it would like
Being supported by the Trust can win you positive publicity	A lot hangs on the relationship you forge with your mentor

Business angels

Business angels are the funders most people dream of meeting. Popular TV programmes show entrepreneurs pitching to panels of investors. Business angels are different from other lenders in that they:

→ invest in the potential as much as what's already achieved;

→ take a share in the business in return for their investment;

→ often get personally involved, helping you to build the business.

Business angels can be hard to find and difficult to approach. Most only invest in business sectors they understand. Many join networks such as **www.nban.co.uk,** but many more work alone, relying on accountants and other intermediaries to broker introductions.

Good points:	Bad points:
Their investment and support can enable you to grow a business quickly	They usually take a significant equity stake in your business. It's no longer all yours
You can end up rich	Angels usually want to sell as soon as they can be sure of getting a good return

Danger!

If you give up too much equity in order to secure investment, you may find yourself no longer in control of your business.

Frequently asked questions

Here are some questions frequently asked by new entrepreneurs about finding funding for their businesses.

I've got a well-paid job, young family, large mortgage and modest savings. I hate my job and want to work for myself. How can I borrow enough to start the business and pay the bills for the first six months?

You probably can't! Consider starting your business part-time and negotiate a gradual reduction in the hours you work for your employer. Many would prefer a phased transition to a shock resignation. Minimise your personal risk by taking it one step at a time.

My dad has offered to lend me the money I need, but I feel a little embarrassed taking it and feel I'm somehow taking advantage of him. What should I do?

I'd take him along to a solicitor or accountant and draw up a proper agreement between you. Is it a loan or a gift? Do you want him to have a share of the business? What's going to be most tax efficient for him? Document the deal and treat it as you would an investment by a stranger.

I'm about to open a themed restaurant and have been offered a grant if I set the business up in a neighbourhood undergoing regeneration. What would you do?

I'd open the business where I thought the most customers would patronise it. Grants can reduce costs, but being in the wrong location can make even the best-funded business fail. Consider the risks and follow your instinct.

If doing all this sounds like a lonely proposition, take heart – there is an ample supply of advisers and mentors available, as you will find in the next chapter.

Key points

→ It's better to have too much money than too little. Be realistic when working out start-up costs. You're only fooling yourself if you under-estimate your need.

→ Success is all about profit. The more profitable your business, the more cash it will generate to fund growth.

→ Cash flow is king. Never let doing the work distract you from getting paid on time.

Next steps

What action will you take to apply the information in this chapter? By when will you do it?

_____

_____

_____

_____

Advisers and mentors and why they're important

Chapter Nine

It is human nature not to seek help. People sometimes see it as an admission of weakness to ask for advice. They choose to battle on alone instead.

In business, as well as in other aspects of life, the opposite is more usually the case. It can take huge strength to ask for help when you're beginning to flounder. The majority of the most successful entrepreneurs you meet will tell you they readily sought advice at critical points in their business career. However, it's important to get advice from the right people.

Never trust the advice of a man in difficulties. AESOP

What does a good business adviser really do?

Research shows that when entrepreneurs do look for advice, the first place they visit is their local bar. Friends and acquaintances are the people most likely to be asked to offer inspiration to the new entrepreneur facing a challenge.

Sometimes they have the answers, particularly if they happen to run their own business and have faced similar obstacles themselves. However, if they do not have business experience but see themselves as experts, their advice can be misleading and potentially catastrophic. Young businesses, rather like babies, are very vulnerable and need lots of loving care.

The best business advice is given by people who:

→ have experienced or solved the problem you are facing;

→ are independent and unbiased by any personal or commercial motive;

→ challenge you to think differently;

→ will stay with you until the issue has been resolved;

→ have integrity, enthusiasm and a genuine interest in your success.

These people may be professional business advisers working for a business support organisation. They may also be freelance consultants who specialise in business start-up and growth. Finally, they may be specialists within an accountancy practice or other business service provider.

How to Start Your Own Business for Entrepreneurs

Being experienced and knowledgeable is not enough. Choose advisers who you can relate to and respect as well. A good adviser gets in close to the business and needs your confidence and trust to be effective.

Case study

Ed Bodiam, SME Advice, www.smeadvice.co.uk

A career providing technology and strategy solutions to small and medium-sized companies gave Ed Bodiam a valuable insight into the challenges business owners face. He set up SME Advice in 2008 to provide 'Virtual Board Members' to his clients as they face change or go for growth.

'I don't try to help unless I know I can, and I only help owners that want to grow their businesses,' he told me, going on to explain how some people have quite jaundiced opinions of consultants in general. Ed's advice is to look at what a consultant has achieved with others before taking at face value what they claim to be able to do for you.

'Much of the value of using an external consultant as a sounding board and mentor is in the discipline it imposes on you,' he explained. 'You are far less likely to let things slip.'

Just why is an outside opinion so important?

Every good entrepreneur lives and breathes their business, certainly for the first year or so. They take an almost obsessive interest in every aspect of the organisation they are building. This determination to suc-ceed is positive, but the downside is that they may lose objectivity. You can become so close to the trees that you forget you're in a wood.

The input and opinion of people from outside the business can help you remain objective. All you have to do is invite comment and listen to what is said. You do not have to act on everything you hear, but it is important to take on board constructive criticism as well as praise.

Outside opinion can help you develop your business and stay on track. People to consult and listen to include:

- → your partner, who wants to see you succeed;
- → suppliers, who have an incentive to see your business grow;
- → customers, who know better than you what they want;
- → trade associations that benchmark your performance against similar businesses;
- → competitors, who react to the threat you pose to their livelihood;
- → your bank manager, who will spot financial trends before you do;
- → your accountant.

As you can see, the list of people who might offer you business advice is almost endless. However, there is a real danger in asking too many people for advice, in that you will find yourself confused as you try to make sense of it all. Never lose sight of the fact that it is your business, your money and your livelihood at stake. Advice should always be welcomed, but follow it only if your instinct tells you it is right.

Peer support

One of the strengths of the many business and networking groups you might consider joining is their ability to deliver you impartial advice. The advice you receive over a networking breakfast, for example, will not be delivered by an expert but by someone who has perhaps encountered the very challenge you are currently wrestling with. The academics call this peer support.

Every small business owner has an incentive to encourage and support others in the same situation. As your new business grows, you will find a tremendous camaraderie among your fellow entrepreneurs. This is not totally altruistic. A significant proportion of the new business won by the typical small enterprise is introduced or referred. In other words, you will recommend the businesses that you know and they will recommend you.

Case study
Craig Bunday, The Business Club Leicester,
www.the-businessclub.org

When Craig Bunday set up a packaging and design consultancy in 2001 he knew that word of mouth marketing and networking were the ways to build it. He joined his local Business Club and quickly found it could deliver much more than sales leads.

As he explained to me, 'I was able to treat my weekly networking group as my management meeting: my networking referral group became my sales team, my support, and in many cases my friends.'

It was this revelation that networking could deliver so much that prompted him to buy a Business Club franchise. Now his business is to manage the group where this networking takes place. As a franchisee, he also benefits from his new network of peers around the country.

Finding a networking group to join

The Business Club is just one example of the many networking groups you can join. Many franchises are creating in themselves business opportunities for those that buy them. All provide opportunities to discuss business problems and challenges as well as to seek out referrals to build your business.

The networks you join will depend largely on the type of business you are in. For example, if you are in a small community and your customers are local, then a local breakfast and networking group is probably right for you. If, on the other hand, you are a specialist supplier with customers spread across Europe, you might do better to join a national trade organisation.

To find the right groups for you, look at the following sources:

→ **Locally.** To find your local breakfast networking club or chamber of trade. Look online, ask around or talk to the local government economic development team who should be able to guide you.

→ **Regionally.** For specialist sector groups often created by local government to build the capacity and skills of a business sector that is important to the region's economy. Also look for privately run networks that meet the needs of ambitious businesses like yours.

→ **Nationally.** Most types of business have a trade association that you can join. These provide specialist support, training and knowledge specific to the type of business you are running.

→ **Universities.** These often run programmes for growing businesses. They may be set up as 'action learning sets', where a group of like-minded entrepreneurs share and discuss their challenges with an expert facilitator.

Sharing resources

There is much more than just advice, tips and hints that you can share with other entrepreneurs. The value of their advice is that they are facing similar challenges to you – and finding ways around them. Sometimes the solutions and shortcuts they have developed can be of immense value to you, too.

For example:

→ you can share standard documents, such as terms and conditions of trade, employment contracts and confidentiality agreements;

→ if a sales letter is particularly effective for one company, it can be quickly adapted to work for another;

→ spreadsheets and other software calculators and shortcuts can be shared easily making everybody more efficient.

Time saver

Rather than reinventing the wheel, find out who's already got a solution you can borrow or copy.

Case study

David Toohey, The Accountants Circle,
www.accountantscircle.co.uk

David Toohey launched The Accountants Circle in 2007. He had been doing contract work for a number of accountants, using their spreadsheet templates. He found these often clumsy and error-prone.

With his team, David developed a suite of more robust accountancy spreadsheets, which are made available to his members. There are now almost 600 accountants and book-keepers that have joined The Accountants Circle.

The strength of David's company is that it enables accountants to share information and ideas with each other. It also provides members with the templates they need without each of them having to reinvent the wheel all the time. Peer mentoring and support of this kind is always valuable and in this case forms a profitable business.

What is a mentor and how are they different from advisers?

Most truly successful people have used a mentor to guide them along the way. Whereas an adviser may be used to dealing with a specific issue or problem, a mentor takes a more holistic view of you and your enterprise. The relationship you develop with a mentor is usually more open, more frank and longer lasting than a relationship with someone simply giving advice.

A good mentor will encourage you to set goals, reflect on decisions and be objective as you grow your business. In many ways they will share the business journey with you, without taking control, so that you have the benefit of their experience and wisdom to support you.

How to find a mentor

Before you look for a mentor, you need to know the kind of person you are seeking. Mentors usually are:

→ older than you and so in no way competitive with you;
→ more experienced in business than you;
→ better connected, with useful contacts they can introduce you to;
→ people who have failed as well as succeeded (failure can teach much more than success!).

Places to look for a mentor include:

→ The Prince's Trust – which can match you with a volunteer mentor if you are aged under 30 and seek the Trust's help before you start your business.
→ Business support agencies – which often also matchmake between businesses and volunteer mentors.
→ Your local business community – where there may be someone willing to share their experience and take a genuine interest in your success.
→ Your industry sector – where one of the elder statesmen may feel that mentoring you is a good way to stay in touch with the industry in which they have spent their career.

The mentoring relationship

The relationship you have with your mentor can be quite informal, almost social. A mentor can be someone who takes an interest in your personal and business growth. They may be motivated to do this because they enjoy helping others and wish to share some of the knowledge and experience they have gained over the years. It can be very rewarding to steer someone away from the pitfalls into which they themselves have painfully plunged.

If you are running a limited company, it may make sense to appoint your mentor to your board as a non-executive director. This means that they are accepting some legal responsibility for the well-being and performance of the company. You will need to pay them an annual fee, but if you choose the right person this will cost a lot less than you might think.

What is important in a good mentoring relationship is that you and your mentor:

→ meet regularly;

→ discuss all aspects of your personal and business performance;

→ do not avoid constructive criticism;

→ deal with problems as they arise;

→ do not agree with each other just to be polite.

Time saver

Always look for a mentor who is a lot further up the entrepreneurial ladder than you. Do not limit yourself by adopting as a mentor someone only a little further ahead than you. A little of a high-flier's time will be more valuable than a lot of time from an 'also ran'.

Frequently asked questions

The following are some typical questions that new entrepreneurs have about finding and working with a mentor or adviser.

How important are formal qualifications when choosing a business adviser?

There are specific business adviser standards and qualifications against which budding advisers may be measured. However, the most important qualification needed to give effective business advice is for the adviser to have witnessed or experienced the challenges for which you are seeking their help. Also, it must be someone you can trust and whose opinion you will respect.

I've heard mixed reports about Business Link advisers. Should I seek advice from a private consultant rather than a government-funded adviser who may not be so good?

There are literally thousands of Business Link advisers and some will undoubtedly be better than others. Remember that sometimes people do not like what they hear from a business adviser because it is a little too close to the truth! Like bank managers, business advisers often get the blame for their clients' shortcomings.

The market leader in my industry has just sold his company and retired. I'd like to invite him to mentor me but I'm not sure how to go about it.
First, you have to put yourself in their shoes. Will working with you give them the chance to review some of their past successes without the day-to-day grind from which retirement has just released them? Put together a list of benefits to them in helping you and then engineer an opportunity to meet them to discuss it.

Key points

→ Be wary of advice from self-appointed experts. The best advisers are those recommended to you by people you trust.

→ Business networks and relevant user groups can be good sources of free, experience-based advice.

→ Everyone will do better with the support of a good mentor.

Next steps

What action will you take to apply the information in this chapter? By when will you do it?

_____

_____

_____

_____

Timing is everything – how to decide when to start

Chapter Ten

Deciding on the best time to start your business is a challenge in itself. If you spend too much time preparing and prevaricating, you will miss opportunities and potentially run out of money. If you start too soon, you may not be prepared to deal with everything that comes your way. Striking a happy balance is what this chapter will help you to achieve.

> ## Very few things happen at the right time and the rest do not happen at all. HERODOTUS

Why you might want to start up straight away

It is natural to want to be fully prepared before you open the door for business. After all, if you fail to impress your first customers because you are not really ready, word will soon spread.

On the other hand, you need your customers to help you develop the right package of products or services that meet their needs. The big danger is that you will spend ages trying to guess or research what your customers expect of you when actually all you have to do is ask them.

Time saver

Don't waste time trying to guess what your customers will want from you. Ask them!

When Sir Clive Sinclair invented the C5 electric tricycle in 1985 he probably did not do enough consumer research first. To him, the idea of scooting down the road in a battery powered plastic tube was a good one. To the motoring public, and in particular the press, it was not.

The British Safety Council criticised the C5 on the day it was launched, commenting, 'The vehicle is too close to the ground and the driver has poor visibility in traffic.' This gave the press the negative headlines they needed and the C5 was soon history.

How to Start Your Own Business for Entrepreneurs

Had Sir Clive involved the media and various road safety experts earlier, he could have developed the product in a way they could support. It might have been quite different, but it would have stood a far better chance of market success.

Start step by step

The key to starting up straight away is to do it step by step. In other words, don't wait until you are ready for a major launch, but instead start your business a little bit at a time. Crucially, this means that your customers, suppliers and others with influence over your success can be involved early on.

The more you involve other people in the development of your business, the more likely you are to get it right. It is also far less stressful to start your business gradually than it is to start with a bang.

Here are some things you might consider:

→ Work with a potential customer or two to develop and then trial your product or service. This means you have a customer from the very beginning. Those customers will probably cover your costs, and hopefully also give you a small profit. More importantly, you can use them to show others that what you are launching is tried and tested.

→ Start your business before you leave your job. Building your company gradually means that you can do this before you resign. A surprising number of people negotiate with their boss a tapered departure from employment. This means they have guaranteed income while they develop the business and their boss has plenty of time to find and train their replacement. Everybody wins.

→ Open for business with a short list of products and services and then add new ones as the opportunity (and demand) arises. It is fair to say that many people put together an extensive portfolio of products because they want to have something for everyone. Once trading, however, you soon find that 80 per cent of your customers buy 20 per cent of what you do. In other words, if you start with what you know will be most popular, you may never need to do anything else.

Why you might choose to be more cautious

Sometimes there is no alternative to waiting and launching your business with an element of surprise. This is often the case when you are leaving employment and are planning to compete in some way with the company you are leaving (if you do this it is vital that you have taken legal advice as to whether your contract of employment might restrict you in this respect).

You might also choose to delay starting your business because you are worried about falling demand, perhaps caused by an economic downturn. If this is the case, work out how much market share you need to take to be successful and to ensure you can be both competitive and profitable.

In times of economic crisis or market shrinkage it is the big players that have the hardest time. You, on the other hand, do not have the massive overheads and have not had years of good times to make you complacent. Furthermore, when times are tough, people are more likely to shop around. It is easier to launch yourself as a new supplier and be taken seriously in a downturn than in a boom. Unprofitable business for a big company can be very lucrative for a small one like yours.

Here are some other possible reasons for caution:

→ You have to wait for a contract period to expire. Perhaps you are taking over from another distributor, or you need to wait until the terms of your former employment contract can be met.

→ Your business is seasonal and you want to coincide the launch with the peak selling period. It could make more sense, for example, to launch a home improvement business in the spring rather than midwinter.

→ There are changes in the wider world – for example, imminent legislation – that mean you are best advised to wait until a certain date when it will be easier for you than it is right now.

In general it is always better to be trading than waiting. If you do decide to hesitate, make sure the reason is a good one. Sometimes people just make excuses to themselves for putting off until tomorrow what deep down they know they should be doing today.

When do other people start a business and why?

The best time to start a business is when the opportunity presents itself. However, the opportunity may not always be obvious. Equally, convention and the people around you may try to discourage you from what they consider to be the wrong thing to do.

Here are some examples of when people started businesses that might surprise you.

Charles Dunstone was just 25 years old with £6,000 to his name when he set up The Carphone Warehouse. He saw that the market for mobile phones was growing and seized his opportunity.

Anita Patel was rejected by several banks. 'They thought my idea wasn't viable and that I was too much of a risk – our family didn't own the corner shop so therefore I wasn't suited to running a business,' she says. With a grant and loan from the Prince's Trust she proved the bank wrong. Today she owns the market-leading company in the field of Asian wedding planning, event management, PR and ethnic marketing.

Anne Davidson saw a need for a magazine in rural Cheshire where she lives after being made redundant from her job in newspaper advertising at the age of 57. She took advice from PRIME (The Prince's Initiative for Mature Enterprise) and set up a very successful monthly magazine called *My Village News*.

People from all walks of life start businesses – at all ages and usually without as much money as they think they need.

How can you make the best decision for yourself?

The best time for you to start your business will probably seem obvious when you get there. Everyone's situation is different, but usually deep down you know when the time has come to push the button and start trading.

When you look back on the first few weeks and months of your business's life, you may well feel that your timing could have been better. Unfortunately, none of us has the gift of foresight and so cannot predict in advance what will happen in the future.

These points may seem a little philosophical for a guide to starting a business, but it is important to recognise them all the same. One of the worst things you can do is to beat yourself up because, looking back, you wish you had done things differently. Learn to look forward and not back and you'll make more progress.

Frequently asked questions

Choosing the best time to start a business can be difficult. Here are some typical questions.

I have been offered the chance of a lifetime, to be the first distributor in the UK for an innovative new health product. I had intended to stay at work until my children left school, but this really does seem too good a chance to miss. What do you think?

Rather like the number 11 bus, chances of a lifetime can be surprisingly frequent or frustratingly absent. I would advise caution in any deal where you are being pressed to make a decision quickly without having time to really research the opportunity. I am sure that even if you miss this one there will be another one, along later.

My employer is consolidating his business and has really lost enthusiasm for the department I run and the work that we do. Should I try to buy out the activity I manage or should I resign and start afresh?

So much depends on where you are with your personal life and circumstances. If starting a business now is what you want to do and you have the support of your family, it would make sense to open negotiations with your boss. You have nothing to lose by being open about your ambition if the work that you do is no longer considered significant to the future of your employer. Do not let yourself be pushed but rather choose your own time to start.

Key points

→ In general it is better to start your business as soon as you can.

→ Remember that you don't have to start your business all in one go. Do it gradually and reduce the risk.

→ You are never too old or too young to start a business.

→ Your intuition will help you decide when the time is right for you.

Next steps

What action will you take to apply the information in this chapter? By when will you do it?

_____

_____

_____

_____

Finding customers

Part Three

Where to look for the best customers

Chapter Eleven

Customers are the food your business needs to nourish itself. In the same way you need food, you cannot do without customers, and if you don't have enough you soon feel hungry. Also, like food, some customers will fire you up but not really provide any benefit, whereas others will be full of concentrated goodness.

Your challenge is to feed your business with a balanced diet of customers and not exist hand to mouth.

> **Emergencies have always been necessary to progress. It was darkness which produced the lamp. It was fog that produced the compass. It was hunger that drove us to explore.** VICTOR HUGO

What are your marketplace boundaries?

When you start your own business, your marketplace can seem to have no boundaries. Perhaps in your employed life you became used to working in a clearly defined geographic territory, or in a predetermined market sector. Now there is no one to tell you where you cannot go. The choice can be bewildering.

You need to strike a happy balance between focusing on the most obvious and easy to win customers, and acquiring the harder to reach but potentially more lucrative business, too. Here's how to define your marketplace boundaries.

Starting point

The chances are high that you already know your first customers. You may not recognise them as such, but they are there all the same. This is because most people start a business in a place or industry where they already have contacts and some experience. Your first customers could be:

→ previous employers who know you and have confidence in what you do;

→ people you have been doing business with on behalf of your employer who will be keen to support your new venture;

→ family and friends within your social circle who know about your business plan and have encouraged you thus far.

It is not unusual for a new entrepreneur to feel that recruiting their former boss as their first customer is somehow cheating. They wrongly believe that to do business properly you have to sell to people you do not know. As a rule, your first customers should be the people you can sell to most easily. If you're worried about breaking the terms of an employment contract, take legal advice. Contracts often sound worse than they really are.

Geography

The most obvious marketplace boundary is defined by geography. If you run a corner shop, your customers will all live nearby or regularly pass by your door on their way to and from work. If you are an accountant, your clients will mostly live and work within your wider community or have some link with it. Although there is no logical reason why an accountant should not have clients spread all over the country, most are recognised and benefit from building a client base close to home, if only for convenience.

Once you start to specialise, geography becomes less important. For example, if your passion was model railways, you might drive 50 miles to visit a specialist shop. Equally, if you were an accountant specialising in showbiz celebrities, your clients might well be spread all over the world.

When you are looking at the geographical area from which you will recruit your customers, consider the following:

→ How big an area you will have to cover to find enough of the right kind of customers. There is no point in going too far, and not going far enough limits your potential.

→ Which competitors are active within that area and how you are going to win customers from them.

→ Any relevant market trends or changes. For example, if you are a shopkeeper in an area where slums are being replaced by trendy apartments, you might need to revamp your shop and stock higher-quality products.

Face to face or virtual

If you shop at your local bookstore, you will only travel to the closest branch. If you shop on Amazon, the physical location of the retailer is of no interest to you as the transaction is conducted online and the goods delivered to your door. The decision to trade online or face to face is a difficult one. Many companies choose to do both, often starting online and then opening retail outlets as their customer base grows.

As a rule of thumb, you can sell commodities online more easily than added-value products that need interpretation or some degree of personalisation. For example, you would probably buy an MP3 player from a website but visit a shop to buy a guitar.

Case study
Ian Clarke, Pansophix, www.pansophix.co.uk

Ian Clarke developed a passion for organisational consultancy while working for BT. With former colleague Steve Westall he launched a training company in 2004. They provide both face-to-face and online soft skills training to corporate clients.

Most of their clients are large organisations in the public, private and academic sectors. From a big company background themselves, Ian and Steve understand the issues and challenges their clients are facing. They are confident, too, that the training they provide meets the customers' needs.

That said, they have listened to their marketplace, and their customer offering has evolved as they adapt to deliver training in ways in which their marketplace wants to buy it. They started purely online, then added face-to-face training and now are moving into publishing. As Ian told me, 'responsiveness is one of the keys to our success.'

Why you need to look beyond the obvious

To start with, you need to look for the obvious customers. There really is no point in making life difficult. However, it is worth spending a little time looking beyond the obvious. That is where you find the new

How to Start Your Own Business for Entrepreneurs

market opportunities or the customer group you had not previously considered. For example:

→ a hotel situated one hour from an airport can market itself to inbound travellers arriving from other countries;

→ a contract gardening company working for affluent householders might also offer a service to estate agents needing empty or neglected properties to be tidied up;

→ a tourist attraction might offer itself as a corporate hospitality venue during the winter when it would otherwise be closed.

Established businesses often discover these new opportunities by chance. An unusual order or approach from someone unlike your typical customer can alert you to the fact that people have found new ways to use what you sell. If you receive an unusual request from a prospective customer, take the trouble to find out what it is they had in mind. Then you can make them the first of many.

Not all of these will be things you want to encourage. For example, young people who sniff glue will not be welcome customers in any DIY store!

Why you need to keep looking when you're busy

If you are going to be working on your own, as most new entrepreneurs do, you will inevitably find yourself incredibly busy at times. It can be difficult to continue searching for new customers when you are overwhelmed with business.

The fact is that the time you are busy is when you have to look harder for new business. This is because new customers often take time to recruit and you want to avoid having a large gap between completing your current projects and starting the next batch.

When you talk to established businesspeople they will sometimes talk about 'feast or famine'. This is a cycle that they fall into, where they are busy selling, then busy delivering what they have sold, then lacking in new customers for a while until they have recruited new ones.

The most successful entrepreneurs are those that continue to sell all the time. Always allocate some time for finding new customers, however busy you are.

You're never too busy to look for new business. In fact, the best time to look for new business is when you're busy. People like doing business with these peope! Be sure to allocate some time every week for this process to keep the flow of customers coming.

How can you do this easily without spending too much?

There are plenty of market research companies and other consultancies eager to sell you their services. As your business grows, you may well find it worthwhile engaging experts to help you identify and reach out to new markets. For now, though, it makes sense to do things yourself. The following are some simple techniques you might try:

→ Look for published customer lists on competitors' websites. These can give you an insight into the kind of customers you could aim for.

→ Visit shopping centres if you are in retail to see what kinds of people shop in outlets like yours. Don't be afraid to stop and question the occasional person and to be honest about why you are conducting research.

→ Search for your own products or services on the internet. You might be surprised by what you find.

→ Survey your first customers to find out how they found you and what they like or dislike about what you do. If encouraged, they can suggest places and people you might consider in your quest for new customers.

→ Once you are trading and marketing your business, use offer codes or simply ask your customers how they heard about you. You can then look for more people from the same source.

Case study
Jude Robinson, Iona Cosmetics,
www.ionacosmetics.co.uk

A back problem meant that Jude Robinson had to give up her work as a doula (supporting women through pregnancy and birth). Because the products could easily be stored and distributed, and also because it was something she understood, Jude started selling cosmetics.

The ranges she distributes are handmade and of a high quality. They are not cheap. She attracts buyers to her website by being very active on a number of social networking websites. She also blogs and has recently started sending out a monthly newsletter.

Using offer codes, Jude tracks the source of orders placed and works out which networking sites deliver the best return. She focuses her efforts on those, making sure that her time is well spent.

Frequently asked questions

Here are some of the questions new entrepreneurs ask about finding customers.

My business will supply and fit carpets in people's homes. Everyone is therefore a potential customer. How can I define my market, and where should I start?

It makes sense to concentrate on one particular type of home or person. Perhaps you could concentrate on your immediate neighbourhood so that your customers are close together and will soon see you as the local carpet fitter. In other words, grow a reputation quickly by working locally.

I like restoring classic cars and had been asked by my uncle to take over his motor engineering business. It is in a rural village, and so apart from a few stalwart customers, finding new ones will be difficult. Any suggestions?

This is definitely an opportunity to focus on classic cars and attract customers from far and wide. I know of a village garage which has survived only by focusing almost exclusively on Volkswagen Beetles. Not only does the business restore and repair old Beetles, but it also has a thriving online business in parts and accessories.

I want to sell fashion accessories online. I'm pretty confident I can get the right products into my range, but how can I define and, more importantly, reach my market?

Your website will be one of thousands selling similar products to the world at large. To succeed you will have to focus. You can focus either on one particular kind of customer – for example, young mums who are too busy to go out to the shops – or on one kind of product. To offer everything to everyone will not enable you to build a relationship with your customers.

Key points

→ Your first customers need to be those that are easiest to recruit.

→ Do not pass potential customers on your way to find new business further afield.

→ Specialising makes it easier for you to find (and be found by) new customers.

→ If you start an online business, don't rule out working face to face once you've built a customer base.

Next steps

What action will you take to apply the information in this chapter? By when will you do it?

_____

_____

_____

_____

How to develop the right brand and image

Chapter Twelve

Your appearance, experience, accent and behaviour define your personality. It is these characteristics and the perceptions they create in the minds of those around you that will help people decide whether or not they want to know you better. Your new enterprise will also develop a personality. The personality of a business is called its brand.

What is brand?

To most people brands are synonymous with the products they represent. That is because most brand awareness is created by people who are marketing consumer products. The marketer develops logos, jingles and advertising campaigns that build and reinforce the aspects of their product that they want you to appreciate and value.

A well-managed brand will use marketing techniques and campaigns to focus the consumer on recognising its key points of difference. For example, Volvo cars have always positioned themselves as being very safe. BMWs, on the other hand, are seen as something to aspire to, that surprisingly is just within reach. Finally, Hyundai focus on the fact that they are usually cheaper than the better known brands of motor car.

When you start a small business, you do not have the budget to create artificially the customer perceptions and beliefs you wish to encourage. That does not mean that developing and managing your brand is not important. It means you have to do things differently.

If you are the entrepreneur launching a new company, it will almost inevitably share many of your traits and values. That is because you have had the original idea, developed the plan and created the organisation. As your business grows it literally takes on a life of its own, giving yours back to you. Managing the transition can be difficult, but that is where your business begins to acquire real value as it is no longer perceived to depend on you for its success.

In great affairs men show themselves as they wish to be seen; in small things they show themselves as they are. NICHOLAS CHAMFORT

Case study
Anna Burns, Eco Emporia, **www.ecoemporia.com**

Anna and Peter Burns took a year out to travel around the world when they got married in 2006. They knew that when they returned they would want to start a business. The business was planned en route.

The couple were committed to reducing their personal environmental impact on the world. It made sense to start a business that helped others to do the same.

In Australia they chanced upon a shop selling craft and gift products made exclusively from reused material. This was the 'eureka moment' that led to the formation of Eco Emporia. The website strapline summarises what the customer can expect to find: 'desirable objects from discarded things.'

Why you need to get your brand and image spot on

However small your new business, you want it to look attractive to prospective customers. You also want the customers you recruit to talk positively about your products or services to people they know. Word of mouth is the most powerful way in which news of your enterprise will spread. Having a strong brand and clear image will help achieve that.

The following are some key elements of branding that will take you in the right direction.

Focus

The more specific your customer proposition, the easier it will be for people to recognise it. For example, imagine you are a motor engineer with a garage in a small town. You repair and maintain cars. If you promote yourself as being able to do anything to any make of any age, you will attract some customers. Probably most will be people looking for someone convenient and close by.

However, if you want to attract customers from further afield, you will need to specialise. Furthermore, as a specialist, your business name and the whole customer experience will need to be tailored to fit your specialism.

If your expertise and inclination encouraged you to specialise in high-performance sports cars, you might set your business up to look like a racing track pit stop – somewhere people go to have highly complicated tasks completed quickly and efficiently.

If, however, you decide to focus on women drivers, you would create a much softer and non-threatening environment. You would set out to demonstrate how you can be trusted. You would also add such services as free collection and return so that the female drivers you work for do not have to come to your workshops.

As you can see, the same business focused on different market sectors might have a completely different look, name and package of services and serve a completely different customer group.

Name

The name you give your business should make it very clear what your business does. Ideally it should convey some benefit message as well. If, for example, a florist's shop is named after its owner, say 'Smith's', you would have to see the shop to know what it does. A better option would be to call it something like, 'Beautiful Blooms', or even 'Flower Arrangers' Heaven', if it sells flowers and the accessories used by people keen on flower arranging.

How to Start Your Own Business for Entrepreneurs

Make it obvious from your business's name what it is you do and how you are different. People can be slow on the uptake, so make it easy for them!

Appearance

Appearance in terms of brand means much more than just your logo. You will know that many major brands are recognisable from only their logo. The Nike 'tick' is a good example, and the McDonald's golden arch is another. A glimpse of either immediately creates in your mind an expectation of what will be delivered by the company behind the logo.

A new business, by definition, does not have an established brand or logo. You have to concentrate on creating good first impressions so that your customers come back time and again. Of course, a good logo can help, but in reality it is what your customer sees that you have to get right. Consider the following examples:

→ **Colour**. The paint on the walls, the fascia of your shop, the clothes you wear and the letterhead on which you send your mailshot all need to be the right colour for the business you are in. Just as a funeral director would not adopt bright red as their house colour, so a trendy design company should not look black and sombre.

→ **Light**. Nightclubs are dimly lit to create ambience and atmosphere. Bookshops are brightly lit so that people can read before they buy. Even a solicitor's office can be lit in such a way that it reassures and comforts the nervous customer, anxious to get a contract worded correctly. Think of your business as a theatre and light it appropriately for what will take place there.

→ **Sound**. The right background music can set the scene of the transactions you wish to conduct. It has been proven in retail outlets that the right background music will encourage people to stay longer and spend more. Equally, banging, crashing and swearing from a workshop adjacent to the room in which you meet customers will not encourage them to buy what is being manufactured next door. Think about what your customers hear.

→ **Smell**. Just as the smell of freshly brewed coffee and recently baked bread will help you to sell your house or flat, so, too, will your business benefit from smelling sweet. If nothing else, always have fresh flowers and fruit on your meeting room table.

Buying design

Most businesses, established and new, depend on graphic design to communicate their brand messages clearly to their audience. The style in which you first alert your prospect to the opportunities you offer should be reflected in every aspect of your customers' experience. From initial mailshot to delivery of the product or service, there needs to be a consistency of image and style.

Graphic design is one of those businesses that it is very easy to start. Consequently, you will find all sorts of design companies when you start looking. This can be confusing. You have to choose between the expensive, established and highly professional design agency and the cheap and cheerful, recently started, young designer who works from home. Here are some tips to help you get the best value when buying design:

1 **Know what you want**. Without a clear idea of what you want your prospects and customers to know about you, think about you and do as a result of becoming aware of you, your marketing will fail.

2 **Write a brief**. Write a single page that details your marketing objectives. What exactly do you want the designer to produce and how will you measure the success of their work?

3 **Find three designers**. Ask people you know to make recommendations, or find out who produced work which has particularly impressed you.

4 **Meet them**. When you meet each designer, give them the opportunity to talk you through their work portfolio, then invite them to comment on your brief. Remember that designers are creative people and you need to give them every opportunity to create ideas for you. Most designers will produce some visuals to illustrate what they can do. They do not expect to be paid for these, appreciating that this is part of the selling process.

5 **Choose one**. Your choice of designer should not be made purely on price. Stunning, innovative design that really positions your business should generate you more profit and therefore be worth paying a premium to acquire.

6 **Let them do their job**. The biggest problem designers encounter with new clients is where the client wants to be totally involved in the project. Of course, it is important that you see the work develop and that you are consulted when decisions are to be made. But do not inhibit your designer by micro-managing the project. Give them enough leeway to surprise and impress you.

Time saver

The clearer you make your brief, the better the designer will translate it into images and the fewer drafts will need to be done.

A sample design brief

For an example, let's say you run a health and safety consultancy. You have 20 years of experience as a government inspector. You know that very few businesses will willingly volunteer to invest in health and safety advice; most think that they can sort it out for themselves and that hiring a consultant will somehow lead to them spending a lot of money on upgrading their facilities.

You want to position yourself as a gamekeeper turned poacher. By paying you to look at a business and tell them what they don't need to do as well as perhaps what they do need to do, you will set yourself apart from your competition. Based on this, you want to be seen as:

→ a 'recycled' inspector who knows how inspectors think;

→ independent and not interested in selling anything apart from your time;

→ determined to save your clients money, not spend their money;

→ qualified and up to date.

You will need stationery, a website and perhaps a simple leaflet.

Winning words

As well as choosing a descriptive and memorable name for your business, there are many other ways you can use words to give your enterprise a boost. Straplines and slogans, for example, can convey the benefits you offer in a very effective way. The words you use in your promotional material need to be clear and concise and written with the reader in mind.

When I make a word do a lot of work, I always pay it extra. RENE MAGRITTE

Here are a few techniques you might consider:

→ **Straplines**. These can benefit hugely from being short and succinct, using techniques such as alliteration (where all words start with the same letter) – for example, 'Brunch on Betty's Bumper Buffet'. Similarly 'Mr Nuisance Pest Control' is effective because pests are a nuisance.

→ **Context**. If you know where your words will be read, you can tailor them to that situation. For example, you could have great fun with an advert for smoke detection on the back of a bus.

→ **You**. This is one of most the powerful words in the English language. Too often new entrepreneurs write about what 'we' do rather than how 'you' will benefit. For example, 'We have the widest range of car batteries in town' versus 'Whatever you drive, you will find the new battery you need here.' The point is that the customer only wants one battery and is not interested in the other 500 you have in stock.

How to Start Your Own Business for Entrepreneurs

Poorly written copy can damage your business. If you find writing words to describe your business difficult, ask someone else to do it for you. PR agencies are one option; another might be as simple as one of your neighbours who is a budding novelist.

Danger

Frequently asked questions

The following questions show some of the concerns new entrepreneurs have about branding.

Brand is difficult for us because our business is totally unique. No one else does what we do and it is difficult to describe easily what the customer can expect. What should we do?

If your business really is so specialised and your customers have nothing to compare it with, you should consider using a metaphor. In other words, compare your business to something the customer is familiar with and will understand. For example, a specialist cleaning company that undertakes difficult tasks could describe itself as a firm of cleaning commandos.

We are taking over an existing business and feel rather stuck with a name we would not have chosen ourselves. There is a customer base and we don't want to risk losing it by changing the name. Any ideas?

There are two things you can do to show that the business is now different, but has not lost the essence of what it was before. The first is to place the word 'new' in front of the name. The other is to add a strap line that clearly defines how the business is now different. Both can be quite effective.

I bought some desktop publishing software for my PC and plan to create my own logo and literature. Surely this is a sensible way to keep costs down?

If you are a talented graphic designer and objective enough to step back from your business and see it through the eyes of others, then yes, producing your own promotional material can save you money. If, on the other hand, you are worried about the professional image you are going to project and would welcome creative ideas from others, you should hire a designer.

Key points

→ Even if you're setting up a one-person company, brand is important. It's how you encourage people to see you in the best light.

→ Choose a name for your business that makes it obvious what you do and why you're different from the competition.

→ Prepare a clear brief before hiring a graphic designer to work on your image. This will ensure that you really work out what you want.

Next steps

What action will you take to apply the information in this chapter? By when will you do it?

_____

_____

_____

_____

How to Start Your Own Business for Entrepreneurs

Your winning marketing message

Chapter Thirteen

Your marketing messages are the words you will use to communicate what you do to your target audience. These messages have to be simple to understand and make it clear that doing business with you is beneficial. They also have to be reflected in what your customer sees and experiences.

Unless you are in retail, your marketing messages will usually arrive in front of your prospective customers without you being there to explain what they mean. This is why the messages need to be clear and consistent. Your message has to be powerful and persuasive enough to encourage your prospective customer to seek more information.

Marketing messages are what you say and write about your business proposition. They are also words and phrases others will remember and pass on when speaking about your business. Memorable marketing messages can help build the reputation of your business. The cynic might describe this as propaganda. But there is nothing wrong with propaganda, providing it is telling the truth.

 The market can stay irrational longer than you can stay solvent. JOHN MAYNARD KEYNES

What makes a good marketing message?

Imagine walking into a hardware store and asking to buy four candles. The man behind the counter hears you ask for fork handles. You both become increasingly frustrated at your inability to communicate. This situation was very funnily communicated by TV show *The Two Ronnies* in 1976. More than 30 years later people are still laughing and talking about the sketch. But it also carries an important lesson: a good marketing message is one that can be easily understood by the people you are trying to influence.

You must remember that people are not always rational, so you have to deliver your message to them in words they will interpret in a positive way. In other words, you have to say it like your customers say it – even if you say it differently!

A good marketing message is:

→ explicit and easily understood by everyone;

→ very descriptive of the positive aspects of what you are offering;

→ memorable and therefore easy to relate to other people.

The concentrated message

Here are three advertising straplines. These are the most concentrated form of marketing message:

> *'Nothing runs like a Deere.'* – John Deere Tractors
> *'Go to work on an egg.'* – UK Egg Marketing Board
> *'I think therefore IBM.'*   IBM computers

Each of the three examples makes it easy to remember the product name. In their way they each also convey a product benefit.

There are other places where you need to use your marketing message. These include:

→ in the names you choose for your business and your products and services – for example, 'Ron's Reliable Taxis';

→ on the signs you place outside your building – for example, 'Welcome to the home of good taste in home furnishings';

→ on all of your brochures and other sales materials.

Danger!

If your team, industry or business sector has its own acronyms, do not be tempted to use them extensively in your marketing messages. Assuming that your audience will understand 'industry speak' is dangerous.

What are the best words to use?

To the reader, the most compelling words in the English language are 'you' and 'yours'. Using these words extensively shows that you are thinking about the reader and not yourself. Put this book down for a moment and look at a promotional website or leaflet. More often than not the writer has written about themselves. It can be offputting, can't it?

Which of the following two versions of a marketing message do you think is more effective?

'We pride ourselves on our ability to make really tasty cakes which we know everyone will enjoy.'

'You will really enjoy our tasty cakes, baked with pride for your satisfaction.'

There is also a lot to be said for using everyday language when describing your business and its activities. You may feel that you do not have a wide enough vocabulary to do your business justice. But people too often find themselves using large and obscure words to describe a simple business proposition. Put yourself into your customers' shoes and use the words you think they will most easily understand.

 Any word you have to hunt for in a thesaurus is the wrong word. There are no exceptions to this rule.

STEPHEN KING

Marketing messages are more than just words

Your marketing message is the way you communicate your brand and its values to your audience. Words are just one aspect of this.

To be effective, every aspect of your business has to reflect those words you have chosen. So, if you claim to be reliable, your business has to emphasise that reliability in every thing that it does. You may even need to exaggerate your promise to make sure the message sticks. For example, if punctuality is part of your message, then a

How to Start Your Own Business for Entrepreneurs

'money-back if more than five minutes late' promise will really reinforce that message.

Case study
Alex Elderfield, Quickstride, www.quickstride.com

Alex Elderfield was frustrated at not being able to book appointments online easily. As a web developer, he knew this should be simple. He reckoned that event organisers and small businesses would welcome the opportunity to be able to accept bookings online more easily.

His business adviser encouraged him to research his idea and to be specific when branding the services he planned to develop. Research revealed two opportunities.

The Event Thing, www.theeventthing.com, makes it easy for people to list and attend cultural and social events. Open Your Diary, www.openyourdiary.com, enables business owners to accept appointment requests and fill in their diaries, even when away from the phone.

In both cases, Alex has chosen names that say exactly what each website does.

Why it is important to say it simply, clearly and consistently

Have you ever played Chinese whispers? You whisper a message to the person next to you and they pass it on to the next person along. Finally the message comes back to the person who started it. The message is spoken aloud and everybody laughs at how much it has changed.

An apocryphal example from the First World War of a message changing as it was sent down the line is 'Send reinforcements, we're going to advance', which became 'Send three and fourpence, we're going to a dance.'

You need to minimise the risk of your marketing message becoming distorted as it is transmitted from one person to the next. Worse is the fact that if it is easy to misinterpret your strapline or slogan intentionally to create something amusing or rude, people will do this!

How to work out what to say

Your marketing messages will be most successful if they tell people what they want to hear. The things that people want to hear are the benefits that your products or services will bring to them. In other words, 'what's in it for them'.

Professional marketers call these 'buying motives'. You buy a drink because you are thirsty, or a jumper because you expect to be cold. When you go to the cinema you will choose to see the film that you think will be the most entertaining. You have to write your marketing messages in a way that appeals to one or more buying motives.

Because you make these buying decisions without having tasted the drink, worn the jumper or seen the film, you are basing your judgement on the information that is available to you. That information has been provided by the people marketing those things. The more appealing you can make your product or service appear, the more likely people are to buy it.

A good way to understand buying motives is to remember this mnemonic: SPACED. It summarises the six main reasons why anybody buys anything. Here is what the letters that make up the word stand for:

→ **Security**. How does it make you feel safe? Locks protect you from intruders; braces stop your trousers falling down; the breakfast cereal you ate as a child seems a safer option than one you have never tried before.

→ **Performance**. How well does it do the job? A sports car is faster than a saloon; a larger computer processor will make software run more efficiently; fillet steak is more tender than sirloin.

→ **Appearance**. How good does it look or how good does it make you look? Does the product carry the right designer logo? Does my bum look big in this? Do I like the colour? Has everyone else already got one of these?

→ **Convenience**. How easy is the product to acquire and use? The chewing gum is in a rack next to the till; you can buy refills anywhere; 'we come to you to save you a trip into town'; 'click here to download and pay online'.

- → **Economy**. How far will it go and what value for money does it represent? More concentrated so that you use less and the tub lasts longer; 50 miles to the gallon; affordable, easy to replace wearing parts; the cheapest in town.

- → **Durability**. How long will it last and will you still be here to support it in the future? Tungsten tipped for longer life; bonded for your financial protection; lifetime guarantee; underwritten at Lloyd's.

Appealing to multiple motives

Running shoes are a good example of a product that appeals to all of the above buying motives. They are surprisingly complex, a fact you only appreciate if you're a serious athlete. Here's how SPACED applies to them:

- → Security – cushioned soles to protect your feet.
- → Performance – flexible so that your feet can move freely.
- → Appearance – stylish so that people know you are a serious runner.
- → Convenience – order online and return for free if not completely satisfied.
- → Economy – with the most competitively priced high-performance shoe.
- → Durability – designed to protect your feet for at least 500 miles.

The extent to which each element appeals to the buyer will depend on their priorities. The marketer's challenge is to make the running shoes appeal to as wide a spectrum of runners as possible.

Case study
Dave Wilkinson, ThinkDave.Com, www.thinkdave.com

Dave Wilkinson started his web business when he couldn't find a web designer that he felt comfortable hiring for his then employer. He told me that too many seemed focused on their own needs rather than his as a potential customer.

After testing the water on a part-time basis, he went full-time in 2007 and hasn't looked back since. I will let him tell you why he is so successful: 'I view my relationship with clients to be a personal one. I won't sell a client something they can't benefit from. I spend a lot of time speaking to clients about their business objectives, trying to understand their businesses and making recommendations based on what is already working in the industry. As the majority of my business comes from referrals, I do my best to keep my clients very happy.'

Where and how do marketing messages get used?

It is always good to have a stock of positive marketing messages that can be used consistently in every aspect of your business promotion: from advertising to brochures, from letterheads to shop fronts, from website to product labels. The more people see and hear consistent marketing messages from your company, the more likely they are to remember and act upon them.

Frequently asked questions

Here are some typical concerns new entrepreneurs might voice about marketing messages after reading this book.

Our products are used in so many different situations and we do not want to limit our customers' imagination with specific marketing messages. How can we get around this?
The answer is to make that very point your point of difference. For example, 'The versatility of our product is limited only by your imagination' summarises your point perfectly.

I started my business to do what I want to do, in the way that I think is right, to make money to support me and my family. Why shouldn't I be proud of that and talk about my ambitions in my marketing messages?
The fact is that your customers will be more interested in themselves than they are in you. Even if your motivation is entirely selfish, your marketing messages need to focus on what your customers will gain from doing business with you.

How to Start Your Own Business for Entrepreneurs

You use the word propaganda in this chapter. Why can't I spread negative information about my competitors as a way of encouraging people to do business with me?

You need to be aware that an awful lot of people take a very dim view of businesses that are critical of their competition. Your customer wants to know that you are ethical, honest and focused on being better than your competition. You may not get this across very clearly if you insist on doing the competition down.

Key points

→ Describe your business in a way that your customers will understand and value.

→ Develop a simple, benefit-focused strapline and use it everywhere.

→ Avoid jargon and acronyms at all costs

→ Remember that 'you' is one of the most powerful words in the English language.

Next steps

What action will you take to apply the information in this chapter? By when will you do it?

_____

_____

_____

_____

How to make sure your website is a winner

The internet plays an increasingly important role in the way all businesses operate. People wanting to know about your business will look at your website before making contact. They will also search the internet for any other information that might be posted there. Customer reviews, comments on blogs, financial information about you and your business and even the size of the mortgage you owe on the family home can all be quickly and easily discovered.

Make your website a winner and also manage your online reputation – and the internet will work for you.

 Design is not just what it looks like and feels like. Design is how it works. STEVE JOBS

What can the internet do for you?

The internet can enable you to reach customers you would never otherwise recruit. A good website will enable you to attract business from anywhere in the world. It can also make it easier for your existing customers to buy from you. Tesco, for example, invested heavily in creating an online superstore where you can do your week's shopping and have it delivered to your door. Tesco's online shop saw 20 per cent sales growth in 2008.

Your website can do things that you could not possibly otherwise achieve:

→ People can find out about your business and maybe buy from you at any time of the day or night.

→ You can update your website at a moment's notice so that people can have access to the latest information, offers and opportunities straight away.

→ Your website can allow you to punch well above your weight. A small company with a good website can appear far more professional than a large company with a poor website.

→ Your website can collect contact details of people interested in your products or services. You can then send them regular updates by email at minimal cost.

→ You can develop a specialist business and market it effectively in
ways that would just not be possible offline.

Case study
Roz Mita, Mannakin, **www.mannakin.co.uk**

Roz Mita admits that she has always been working on one business idea or
another. She ran a successful African art company for ten years and then a web
and publishing business in Malawi.

Back in the UK, she was working in retail consultancy when she spotted a
gap in the mannequin market. Her company buys and sells used mannequins
and parts, as well as restoring damaged dummies back to pristine condition.

Half of her work comes via Google and the rest by word of mouth. Roz
spends a lot of time maintaining her search engine rankings so that people
searching for mannequins find her first.

Roz's website is her shop and Google her shop window.

Why some websites work and some don't

There are two kinds of website: those that are primarily for entertainment and those that are primarily for the promotion of products and
services. Entertainment websites are used to build loyalty to consumer
products. For example, a fizzy drinks company might create an interactive website with games, competitions and free downloads as part of a
wider marketing campaign.

It is more likely that you want your website to promote your business, gather enquiries and perhaps enable people to buy from you
online. In that case, your website needs to be:

→ focused very clearly on what it is you want people to know and
think about your business;

→ easy to navigate and quick to download;

→ accessible by all your potential customers (a good web design
company can advise you how to achieve this);

→ interactive, so that as many people as possible will leave you their details.

Page layout

There is little point in trying to reinvent the wheel when it comes to web-page layout. You want your website to communicate quickly and effectively, and to do this it needs to present the information where people expect to be able to find it.

If you look at some of the most visited news websites that have con-stantly changing content, you will see that they all follow the same layout. Good examples are the BBC (**www.bbc.com**), the *Financial Times* (**www.ft.com**), *The Economist* (**www.economist.com**) and the *Wall Street Journal* (**www.wsj.com**).

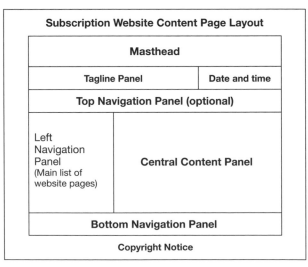

Subscription Website Content Page Layout	
Masthead	
Tagline Panel	**Date and time**
Top Navigation Panel (optional)	
Left Navigation Panel (Main list of website pages)	**Central Content Panel**
Bottom Navigation Panel	
Copyright Notice	

SOURCE: MILES GALLIFORD, **WWW.SUBHUB.COM**

The following are the elements of a successful web page:

→ Masthead across the top. This is where you will find the title of the page and all logos and so on that reinforce the brand.

→ Primary navigation bar down the left-hand side. This navigation bar usually appears across the whole website. It should list all the main categories of the website so that users can find their way around from any page.

→ Time and date – to the right-hand side under the masthead. These show that the website is current, even if automatically updated.

→ Bottom menu bar. This tends to contain links to terms and conditions, privacy statement, site map and so on.

→ The central panel. This contains the main content of the page, including any links to other useful pages.

→ Search box at top right on every page – this enables people to search the entire website.

Make sure that your website contains a site map. This not only provides an alternative navigation for visitors to your website, but is also used by search engines when indexing the site.

Content

Many people choose to create their own website and many more use content management systems to edit their own sites. This means that what you write and paste into your website can go live within minutes. There are many providers of the basic website framework into which you can add your own content. One of the best, which also provides a lot of useful articles, is **www.subhub.com**.

Before adding content to your website it is wise to do the following:

→ Run a spellcheck as it's surprisingly easy to miss typos and spelling errors.

→ Have someone else read what you have written and check that it makes sense to them.

→ Reduce the size (resolution) of pictures so that they download quickly when the page is viewed. If you want people to download pictures you can always have higher resolution versions stored for download elsewhere on the site.

How to get value for money from your website

As a rule of thumb, money invested in a website is money well spent. No organisation is credible without one and a poor website will reflect badly on your business.

If you are tempted to build your own website, factor into your decision the amount of time it will take to do. Make sure you are not building a website to distract yourself from more important things like selling!

Your website will also need regular maintenance, as without new content it will quickly become out of date. Moreover, search engines rank websites according to the frequency with which new content is added. They also look to see how many links are made to your site from others. You need to budget both time and money for this.

The only way you will know whether this is a worthwhile investment is if you set targets for enquiries and orders taken via your website. You can then look at the return on that investment.

Case study

Andy Harris, Custwin, **www.custwin.co.uk**

As a web techie in the dot-com boom, Andy Harris saw plenty of examples of what not to do to succeed in e-commerce. As he told me, 'Numerous businesses went to the wall due to flaky business models and lack of customer focus.'

Andy started writing e-newsletters packed with practical tips and soon found himself being asked to help companies with their web marketing. Although he says that this has become a crowded marketplace of late, he finds that there is still room for people with real experience and expertise.

He has a free downloadable guide to web marketing on his website, but here are his top three tips.

1 Know where your leads are coming from and invest where it's best.

2 Track the way people are using your site and remove obstacles. Andy recommends **www.webstat.com**.

3 Only invest in 'pay-per-click' advertising when your site is already good at converting visitors into customers.

Trading online

There can be little more satisfying than logging on to your computer in the morning and finding that people have been buying from you online.

Not surprisingly, an awful lot of people have set up e-commerce websites – and many of those have rapidly become disillusioned and disappointed. However, providing you have the right offer and your website is easy to find, online trading can be very successful. A good place to start is eBay (**www.ebay.co.uk**). If you are not familiar with this online trading platform it is worth spending some time exploring it. The help section of the website is packed with tips and hints about online trading.

How to sell online

As well as selling your products or taking bookings for services, you can sell downloadable products such as software templates and podcasts. Remember that people will buy anything that saves them time and money.

If you are selling physical goods, you do not necessarily have to hold them in stock yourself. There are fulfilment specialists who will warehouse your inventory and dispatch it to your customers on your behalf as each order is received.

To enable e-commerce, you need to have a shopping cart and secure payment processing integrated into your content site. The shopping cart enables buyers to select one or more items to buy and then takes them through the checkout process.

The payment processing can be done via a 'payment service provider' such as PayPal (**www.paypal.com**).

If you are expecting to do a lot of online business it makes sense to set up your own merchant account with a bank. PayPal is cheaper to use if you have fewer transactions. Once your online business grows, it will cost you less to set up a merchant account with a bank. Remember that payment service providers make their money by taking a percentage commission on each transaction made.

There are lots of online trading platforms that you can add to your website or access from it. Research the options thoroughly before making your choice.

Other money-making options

As well as the obvious products and services, there are other ways you can make money from your website. These include the following:

→ **Advertising**. You can encourage non-competing businesses to buy banner advertising on your site. Easier to manage and less intrusive are text advertisements that contain links to the sponsor's website. You can easily add these to your website via **www.google.com/adsense.**

→ **Affiliates**. You promote another business on your website and earn a commission when people click through and buy. The best-known example of this is **http://affiliate-program.amazon.com/gp/associates/join.**

→ **Subscriptions**. People pay a monthly fee to access specialist content on your website. You set your site up to have a members only area that only subscribers can access.

Danger!

If a product or service won't sell offline, it is unlikely to be a success online. Where possible, make sure people want what you're offereing before marketing it online.

Spam

Some people play the numbers game by spamming – that is, sending huge numbers of emails advertising a product. This method is noted for being used by distributors of illegal pharmaceuticals and various sex aids. Many servers filter out such mass mailing. This way of conducting business does nothing for your reputation and little to build customer loyalty, and in some cases it is illegal. In the UK, regulations enacted in 2003 state that online marketers can send email pitches and SMS messages only to consumers who have agreed beforehand to receive them, except where users are existing customers of a particular company. Don't spam!

Frequently asked questions

The following are questions that new entrepreneurs often ask about websites.

We've set up a website but it does not seem to be attracting much traffic. How can we get more people to visit our website?

There is a real science to the art of attracting traffic to a website. There are obvious things you can do, such as adding the words to your website that the search engines look for (these are known as 'key words'). Many website templates provide boxes into which you can type the key words that you think people would use to search for the product or service you offer. If this is confusing, it might be worth asking your web developer to introduce you to a 'search engine optimisation' specialist. These are people who make their living helping others attract visitors to their website.

A friend told me that the more generic I can make the domain name then the more likely it is that people will find my website easily. Is this true?

Personally, I would not spend a lot of money buying generic domain names. I would prefer to invest in good-quality search engine optimisation (see previous answer).

We have set up our website with a fantastic content management system. The problem is that we never seem to have time to update it with new content. Have you any tips?

What you need is a freelancer, ideally with journalism training, who can interview you regularly to find out what you need on your website and then write and post articles on your behalf. Look for someone affordable, literate and with an eye for detail.

Key points

→ Your website is your shop window to the world, so make sure it projects the best possible image of your business.

→ Remember that your time may not be best spent fiddling with your website. Do not be slow to hire professional help.

→ Experiment with e-commerce using eBay and PayPal before investing large amounts of money in a full e-commerce web solution.

Next steps

What action will you take to apply the information in this chapter? By when will you do it?

_____

_____

_____

_____

How to get good PR and keep on getting it

Chapter Fifteen

People believe what they read in the newspapers, hear on the radio and see on TV. Becoming part of the news is what public relations (PR) is about. What's more, compared to the cost of advertising, PR can represent good value for money. Being reported positively in the press is very good for your credibility.

The skill of getting your business in the press is to put yourself in the editor's shoes. Your story needs to be presented in a form that they will readily see is newsworthy and of interest to their readership.

The first thing to do if you want to publicise your business in this way is to read the publications, listen to the radio stations and watch the TV channels that your customers are watching. Get to know which journalists cover the kind of topic your story might be about. Cut out and keep stories about competitors and start to see what makes a good news story.

> ## There is no such thing as bad publicity except your own obituary. BRENDAN BEHAN

What is PR really all about?

People have an innate preference for the familiar. They are reassured by familiar brands and will stay with one supplier until something goes wrong, or until you come along and persuade them to try something different.

PR is all about building awareness of your business, your products and services and yourself. It is by making people familiar with your enterprise that you will encourage them to do business with you.

Never underestimate the importance of building and maintaining your personal profile among your customer community. People buy from people – and you want people to buy from you. Many new entrepreneurs are coy about seeking personal publicity but really they should not be.

Here are a few examples of the power of publicity and PR:

→ Good press reviews will encourage more people to go to see a film.
→ Businesses will enquire about new software that they have read about in their trade press.

→ People will visit a new shop if a celebrity is cutting the ribbon.

→ A news story about how an alternative therapy has helped someone deal with a health problem will encourage other sufferers to telephone that therapist.

How journalists think and what they like to see

Journalists want to fill their publication with interesting news that is relevant to their readership and encouraging to their advertisers. The more specialist the publication, the more important it is that the content is specifically focused on the readership.

In general journalists are looking for stories that are:

→ interesting – to current and potential readers;

→ exclusive – and not available in any other publication (in the same form);

→ current – in other words, about something that is happening right now;

→ trendsetting – breaking new ground and potentially going to grow;

→ valuable – offering helpful advice to the readers.

Journalists also expect to be supplied with stories in a form that they can use. In other words, they prefer an emailed Word file or the text pasted into the body of an email so that it can be lifted out, edited and pasted into the publication. This is because some journalists also make up the pages of their publication. By providing the text ready to paste, you are making life easier for them.

Do not underestimate the importance of submitting a well-presented, well-written news release accompanied by a professionally taken photograph. If your press release doesn't cover all that it should, it may not get used, as few journalists will have the time for further research.

A newspaper consists of just the same number of words, whether there be any news in it or not.

HENRY FIELDING

What journalists regard as news

News is all a matter of context. You might have won the biggest order of your life, but if last week's paper featured your competitor with an order ten times the size, your story will not be regarded as news.

If, on the other hand, you have just managed to persuade the producers of a TV soap opera to use your products as props in the programme, then however insignificant the order size, probably it will be regarded as news.

The difference is the involvement of the TV soap opera. All a newspaper's readers will be aware of it and many will watch it. Your ability to link the newspaper with the soap opera makes the story newsworthy.

Of course, the best way to find out what a journalist will regard as news is to pick up the phone and ask. In general, journalists on local newspapers or trade publications are receptive to phone calls from small business owners, particularly if they are brief and to the point. You won't find this works with the national press or with major consumer magazines.

As well as the obvious business successes, new appointments and significant investments that make up the bulk of business news releases, there are other topics that can get you into the media. For example:

→ your expert comment on a current hot topic ('Beards are back in fashion, says local dermatologist, concerned at the damage it causes women's faces');

→ a high-profile event you are organising ('New York model Amy Buffer will be at Anytown boutique Charmers on XYZ to launch their new spring range');

→ 'how-to' tips ('Ten top winter pruning tips by Adam Trimmer from Anytown Garden Centre');

→ human interest stories ('Manchester life coach Bertie Better to climb Kilimanjaro to raise money for leukaemia research');

→ volunteering opportunities ('Matron Mandy Morton is looking for volunteers to decorate her old folks' home with paint and brushes donated by Brighton DIY store Colours').

A few words about photographs

Often the make or break factor in getting your story into the media is your ability to provide a decent photograph. Each of the examples above stands a better chance of success if accompanied by professional photos – for example:

→ a close-up shot of the dermatologist examining damaged skin;

→ a shot of the New York model on the catwalk;

→ a picture of Adam pruning a shrub;

→ the life coach in full mountaineering gear on top of a Manchester landmark;

→ the old folks' home matron pointing out her tatty paintwork, paint and brush in hand.

The easy way to write a press release

Unless you have been invited to provide an article for a newspaper or magazine, you should aim to keep your press releases short. This makes it far easier for a journalist to see what your story is about. If you have a strong story, they will always come back to you for more information, but they prefer not to have to edit down a huge multi-page release into the hundred or so words they have space for.

Press releases work best if they follow traditional and proven formula. Outlined below are the sections of the press release and how to cope with each of them. Let's use an example to illustrate the points. Imagine that you sell and install hot tubs. You have persuaded your supplier to write off an old model that has been in your showroom for a year and is slightly damaged. You have donated it to a local charity that works with disabled children.

Page header

It is always good to make it clear that your document is a press release. The way you do this is by:

- → printing 'press release' in large type at the top;
- → adding 'for immediate release' unless for some special reason the story is not to be printed right away;
- → adding the name, phone number, and email of the person the editor can contact for more details;
- → double spacing the copy on the page so that it is easy to read and the journalist can insert their own notes;
- → using a clear typeface.

Headline

Your release should start with a headline. The chances are that a sub-editor will rewrite a headline if the piece is printed, so focus your headline on impressing the journalist. Make it factual and don't worry if it runs to a couple of lines. For example, 'Donated hot tub provides splashing good fun at children's home.'

First paragraph

The opening paragraph needs to contain everything that you most want the publication to print. In many ways it should be a summary of the whole release. Try to add a quote as these will be reproduced verbatim. In our story it might read like this:

> Top Tubs, Newcastle's leading supplier of hot tubs and Jacuzzis, has just given a hot tub to The Pines home for children with disabilities. 'The children love splashing around in their new tub,' said home Director Zia Kapoor. 'What's more, playing in the jets of warm water really helps them as it soothes painful limbs and encourages them to gain greater mobility.'

The paragraph tells the reader that:

- → Top Tubs is generous and kind;
- → hot tubs are fun;
- → hot tubs are therapeutic and good for aching limbs.

Second paragraph

Next, you need to expand on the story and add some more information about both your company and your motivation. Reveal something of your motivation for what you do. In our example, the second paragraph might read:

> Commenting on the donation, Top Tubs proprietor Jane Smith said, 'I've always promoted hot tubs for their therapeutic benefits as well as because they can be a great place to relax with friends. One of our customers has a disabled child and told me how helpful the tub we sold them was. I wanted more children to have that same experience.'

This paragraph tells the reader that:

→ Jane listens to her customers;

→ she has a generous, caring nature;

→ hot tubs are great for relaxing.

Final paragraph

This is the paragraph that may or may not be included. Use it to provide supporting information and references, as well as more detail if appropriate. Make sure you do not miss out any basic information. A good way to test this is by checking that the five Ws of information are all included in the release somewhere: who, where, when, what and why. In the example, the final paragraph might read:

> Recent research by leading disability charity XXXXXX showed that children with physical disabilities respond well to the soothing properties of warm water. It was reading a report of this research, as well as feedback from parents of a disabled child, that encouraged Jane Smith to make a generous gift to the children's home. The home is close to Top Tubs' showroom on XYZ Drive, Newcastle.

Mark that this is the end of the release with the word 'ENDS'.

Boilerplate

This is a summary of what your business is all about. It is your opportunity to tell what you do and when you were established, as well as a little more about you. It is where the journalist looks for additional information, such as the contact details of the best person to talk to for further information.

In the example above, the boilerplate could also contain hyperlinks to recent independent research that supports the claim that children with physical disabilities benefit from using a hot tub.

Time saver

If you are finding it hard to write your release, concentrate initially on the headline and first paragraph. Once this feels right, the rest will follow. Always set your work aside and read it afresh after a break, or ask someone else to check it before you submit it to a journalist. You can't always see your own mistakes.

Dealing with bad news

Not all the news is good news. When your business faces a major problem that you suspect will be reported in the press, it is usually better for you to be the messenger. For example, if one of your customers suffered a serious injury using your product, or worse on your premises, you may need to make a timely statement to the press in collaboration with your insurer. In some situations you may need to check your legal situation before doing this, and even if you have not used one before, a PR adviser can help you make sure you word your statement appropriately.

The alternative is that the media will report the story anyway, If you don't comment, they will say that you were 'not available for comment', or even 'refused to comment', either of which can have a negative impact on your image.

How to Start Your Own Business for Entrepreneurs

> **Nothing travels faster than the speed of light with the possible exception of bad news, which obeys its own special laws.** DOUGLAS ADAMS, *The Hitchhiker's Guide to the Galaxy*

If you are worried about the possibility of a negative story, seek confidential advice to draft a statement in advance just in case. This will help you to avoid saying the wrong thing under pressure and it could help to 'kill' the story in time if needed. If you don't want the journalist to come back to you again, make sure 'no further comment will be issued at this time' is added at the end.

It's not a good idea to spin bad news.

"A few people have had a mild adverse reaction to our special of the day..."

When to hire a PR agency and how to do it

PR agencies come in all shapes and sizes. It is important to get the right one if you want to publicise your business using professional help. Young businesses often overlook the power of PR, despite the fact that advertising can cost a lot more and achieve a lot less.

Just as you are starting your business, it can be really useful (and more economical) to work with a PR specialist who is also just starting a business.

Here are some of the advantages of using a PR consultant or agency:

→ They already know how to write effective news releases.

→ They will have a network of journalists they can talk to.

→ They may have other clients with whom you can collaborate.

→ They will have experience of damage limitation if things go wrong.

One of the best ways to find the right PR person is to ask the editors of the publications you want to be featured in to recommend someone. They will know who they like working with and who they find intensely annoying.

Frequently asked questions

Below are some of the types of concern new entrepreneurs have about dealing with PR.

Our local business magazine said they would only print our story if we buy advertising. What do you think we should do?
Quite a few small regional business magazines survive only because people pay to be featured in them. The trouble with this is that the reader knows that the story is there because it has been paid for, not because it is necessarily news-worthy. I never pay for editorial coverage in any way.

We had a celebrity open our shop and the local TV channel promised to come along but did not turn up. What did we do wrong?
You probably did nothing wrong. TV camera crews are very busy, and if a bigger story breaks on the day they always go there and give you a miss. Don't be disappointed if they don't show up – and don't stop trying.

You say that photographs are important but I hate having my photograph taken. Is it really that important?
You are the public face of your company and as such it is important that you are seen. Of all the challenges you face starting a business, getting used to having your photograph taken should be one of the smallest.

Key points

→ Editorial coverage is almost always more influential than advertising.

→ Don't overlook TV and radio. There are now hundreds of channels looking for content.

→ Good creative photography really pays off.

→ Bad news cannot be ignored.

Next steps

What action will you take to apply the information in this chapter? By when will you do it?

_____ _____

_____

_____ _____

_____ _____

↑

Marketing in a nutshell

Chapter Sixteen

Marketing is the process by which your products and services move from concept to customer. Marketing is much more than just promotion. It is also the process by which you work out what you are going to sell and at what price.

If you sell the right things to the right people at the right price you will make a profit. If you have the wrong product or service, or sell at the wrong price, you will make a loss.

" **Authentic marketing is not the art of selling what you make but knowing what to make. It is the art of identifying and understanding customer needs and creating solutions that deliver satisfaction to the customers, profits to the producers and benefits for the stakeholders.** PHILIP KOTLER

What is marketing all about?

Your passion, past experience, present opportunity and ambition have driven your decision to start a business in a particular sector or location. You have already looked at your business plan, at how you are different from your competitors and at how you will find and communicate with your customers.

A marketing plan is another chance to make sure that you have not overlooked any important opportunities. It also enables you to check the reality and achievability of your business plan.

There are four elements to marketing, often referred to as the four Ps: products/services, promotion, place and pricing.

Products/services

You have probably already worked out what your products and services are going to be. They are the things you are going to offer that people will pay for. But have you remembered everything? It can be surprising what people will buy.

Here's an exercise that will help you to make sure you're not missing out. Create a table with what you can offer along one axis and the customer types you can most easily reach along the other. Your current or planned products and services should then be plotted on to the table. You may find gaps – and it is filling in these with products or services you might otherwise have overlooked that makes this exercise worthwhile. Let's look at how James, a personal trainer, did the exercise:

	Fitness assessments	Training programmes	Training supervision	Diet advice/ food hampers
Busy people who want to keep fit	X	X	X	
People who want to lose weight	X	X	X	X
People recovering from illness	X	X	X	

James quickly realised that although he was quick to give diet advice and weekly food hampers to those seeking weight loss, his other clients were also potential customers for hampers. The difference was client motive. Rather than wanting a carefully calorie-controlled diet, many of his 'busy people' clients found shopping and cooking a chore. They tended to eat unhealthy fast food too often as a consequence.

He started making up and selling hampers for them, too, containing healthy meals they only had to heat up. This saved them time and ensured they had a healthy balanced diet. James arranged for his wife and mother to do the shopping and food preparation for the hampers as he too was busy working one to one with his clients. This meant he could grow his turnover and profit even when he didn't have time to recruit and work with more training clients.

Remember that everything has a value and that you might be discarding or discounting things you could sell. For example:

→ a cabinet maker bags up his wood shavings and sells to a pet shop;

→ a business consultant sells downloadable pre-formatted spreadsheets that he uses with his clients.

Case study
Anthony Marett, Don't Travel Empty,
www.donttravelempty.co.uk

Anthony Marett runs a coach business and wondered how he could overcome the lost opportunity of his coaches returning empty from the airport once a group has been dropped off to catch their flight.

Research told him that this was a national problem, and while hauliers had specialist brokers who matched empty trucks with one-way cargoes, there was no such opportunity for coach operators.

In 2008 he set up 'Don't Travel Empty' to plug that gap in the market. Not only does it help him keep his coaches full and therefore earning, but he also charges a monthly subscription to other coach operators using his website to find either additional passengers or an empty coach to which they can subcontract a one-way job.

Promotion

The ways in which you promote your products or services to your prospective customers may include using advertising, direct mail, posters, point-of-sale displays in shops, vehicle liveries and websites, among others. The way you configure and combine these different activities is commonly referred to as the marketing mix.

Your marketing mix will largely depend on the type of business you are in. Some of the detail about how to do this can be found in Chapters Eleven to Fifteen, but here the important point to make is that you should measure the effectiveness of all your promotional activity. You can do this in the following ways:

→ By finding out where your enquiries or sales came from. What was it that encouraged the buyer to come to you?

→ By reconciling the cost of promotions with the sales they generate. This means you can focus more money on the activities that deliver the best results.

→ By remembering that word of mouth is far and away the most effective form of marketing and it costs nothing.

Time saver

Diligently measure the results from your promotional activity. Then you can save time and money by focusing on what works for you and ditching the rest.

Distribution (place)

The ways that your products or services reach the market is called your distribution. This is not as straightforward as it might first appear. You have choices to make. For example, imagine that you make decorative cat and dog collars. You can either sell them direct through advertising, events and via your website, or sell them through pet stores.

If you sell direct, you will have a larger profit margin but will have to invest in advertising and promotion. If you sell through retailers, they will do the promotion for you as they already have a customer base. However, they will buy from you at a significant discount from your suggested retail price.

If your vision is to be a small specialist supplier, then selling direct might be the best idea. But if you plan to grow your business, employ people to make your pet collars and need a high volume of sales to keep everything moving, then working with distributors such as pet shops could be the right way forward.

The same model applies to services because you will inevitably pay an introductory commission to people who introduce you to new clients. The alternative is to spend your time and money meeting potential clients in the hope that you meet somebody at the right time.

There are many ways that you can distribute your products and services and you must consider all the alternatives carefully before making your decision. It is also quite common for companies to use more than one of these routes to market. If you do this, you can again evaluate the return on investment in each and adjust your effort and investment accordingly.

We're all working together; that's the secret.

SAM WALTON

Pricing

There are only two ways to calculate your selling price. The first is to total your costs and add a margin. The second is to charge the market value for your product or service. In an ideal world the market value of what you are selling will be a higher price than your costs plus a margin. If it is lower you have a problem.

Let's see how the pricing process works for John, who is setting himself up as a marketing consultant. He plans to sell his expertise to businesses seeking growth and to introduce them to trusted associates who can provide graphic design and web development services. Before being made redundant, John had a salary of £40,000 a year.

His first attempt at calculating a day rate was to divide the number of days he felt he could work in the year (200) by the salary he was used to earning. That gave him a day rate of £200.

His second attempt resulted from his wife reminding him that as a business owner he would have overhead costs. His target income suddenly increased like this:

Salary	£40,000
Car	£10,000
Travel, etc.	£5,000
Home office	£2,000
IT	£1,000
Phone/broadband	£500
Stationery	£1,000
Training	£1,000
Subscriptions, etc.	£500
Total	**£61,000**

This gave him a day rate of £300.

His third attempt involved taking a look at the market rate for marketing consultants of his calibre. He found that small start-up businesses were unlikely to pay much more than £200 a day because they could not afford more than this. Nor could they benefit from all his expertise because they were not yet big enough to grow very quickly.

He then looked at larger organisations needing more complicated, strategic input and found that they would pay £800 a day or more. He realised that if he worked for large organisations for just 100 days a year he would be better off than if he ran himself ragged working with small companies.

Remember that you're in business to make money. Look at all the options before choosing one or more routes to market. Focus on profit, not turnover.

Case study
Andy Forty, DCC Supplies, www.dccsupplies.com

A self-confessed model railway enthusiast, engineer Andy Forty and his son set out to build what they described as a 'proper' model railway. They wanted something sophisticated that would enable them to run trains at different speeds on the same piece of track. Research revealed that a solution existed, but nowhere in the model railway world could Andy buy what he wanted. A business idea was born.

Today, DCC Supplies provides this specialist hobbyist equipment to model railway enthusiasts worldwide. Over time the business has diversified into other markets – for example, enabling Railtrack to create realistic traffic movement simulation for training their staff.

Andy attributes his success to 'old-fashioned market research and sound product choice, followed up by wide product exposure via well designed search engine optimisation, thorough analysis of sales and advertising. All underpinned by good customer service.'

Why is it so important to keep finding new customers?

Running a business is like riding a bicycle. When you stop pedalling, soon you fall over because the momentum that kept you upright has been lost.

To put it another way, a business is either growing or shrinking. There is no equilibrium, although at times it may seem so. You need to constantly recruit new customers because:

→ some will naturally go away over time;

→ you will have disputes and lose some that way;

→ as your business grows, you will outgrow many of your original customers;

→ people retire, die and go bust.

 Your most unhappy customers are your greatest source of learning. BILL GATES

Where to look for help

Getting the right balance with product, promotion, place and price is one of the most challenging tasks you face as an entrepreneur. In an ideal world you would be able to set your own price, or at least make a decent margin by matching market pricing. In reality it is far more complicated.

For example, it is damaging to your profit to overengineer your product or service, adding cost and features that your customers do not value and will not pay for. Equally, if you do not have a sophisticated enough product or service to meet market needs, you'll only be able to compete on price and that is even worse. Striking a happy balance is something you might find easier with outside help.

Most companies that promote themselves as marketing specialists are actually little more than graphic design studios. They usually have plenty of experience of businesses in different marketplaces and therefore can offer some advice. However, they are not specialists in marketing in the sense that you may need.

In the UK, the best place to look for a qualified marketing adviser is through your local Business Link. This government-funded, independent agency maintains a database of advisers in a whole range of business subjects. Your local Business Link can be found via **www.businesslink.gov.uk**.

Time saver

Always seek and listen to independent, expert advice. It'll save you lots of time and potentially some heartbreak, too.

Frequently asked questions

The following questions are typical of the kinds of concern that new entrepreneurs have regarding marketing.

I am an engineer making specialist equipment for the livestock industry. My products are technically far superior to my cheaper rivals, but I am finding it impossible to persuade farmers to pay a premium price for my products. What should I do?

Unfortunately, technical superiority alone will not command a market premium. It is what the additional features deliver in terms of value to the customer that dictates the price they will pay. Doing a better job does not make a bigger profit if your customer, the livestock farmer, cannot see a return on his investment in your equipment. Consider developing a cheaper range.

I find it easy to win customers, but for some reason they tend to buy once and then go away. Very few call me to place a repeat order. Why could this be?

Perhaps it is because you are not asking them to place a repeat order. When you take their initial order, you must know when they will run out and need to replenish their stock. Ring them a week or two before you think they need to order, to ask them how they're getting on and to offer to send the next consignment. The fifth P word not mentioned before is 'proactive'!

We are going to make specialist polishes used by owners of antique furniture. We want to sell through antique dealers and furniture stockists, but each will carry so little stock it is expensive even to think about visiting them all. How can we get around this?

The furniture trade, in common with many others, makes extensive use of freelance sales agents. These independent salespeople work on behalf of a range of suppliers, earning commission on the orders they generate from retailers. You need to find a sales agent whose product range would be enhanced by your range of products.

Selling is another key skill for new entrepreneurs. In the next chapter you'll discover how to make the process easier, even if you find it intimidating.

Key points

→ Marketing is much more than just promotion.

→ Map your market opportunity to identify otherwise overlooked opportunities.

→ Make sure when costing your product or service that you include all costs, especially your own time.

→ Business Link can be a good place to find someone to advise you on getting this right. Sometimes you can qualify for a grant towards the cost.

Next steps

What action will you take to apply the information in this chapter? By when will you do it?

_____

_____

_____

_____

↑ Ways that anyone can be good at selling

Chapter Seventeen

Selling is not as difficult as you might first think. It is not about brow-beating your prospect into submission. Most selling is about having a structured conversation to explore the potential of doing business together.

Naturally your ambition is to get a sale. It should also be your prospect's ambition to make a purchase. If people are not interested in what you are selling, no amount of pressure or persuasion will change them. Equally, if you do not passionately believe that what you are selling is the right solution to your prospect's current challenge, it will show and you will lack credibility.

When you are selling your products or services, you are enthusing others about something you find very exciting. By selling what you do, you will share your vision and your dream, but it has to be their dream, too. Everyone is different, so their motivation for considering a purchase from you will be different. The structure of a sales interview enables you to understand those differences and demonstrate how you have the right solution.

If you are confident that what you are offering is of real value and you are committed to making it work, then you will be good at sales. Conversely, you can have all the sales techniques in the world but no faith in your product and you will fail.

 Do you want to spend the rest of your life selling sugared water or do you want a chance to change the world? STEVE JOBS (When recruiting a soft drinks executive to run Apple)

A few words about buying

In Chapter Thirteen you were introduced to the concept of buying motives. These are the reasons that people buy anything. Your product or service has to satisfy one or more of the following needs: security, performance, appearance, convenience, economy and durability. The buyer may not feel motivated to make a purchase right now, but they will be aware that they have a need. For example:

How to Start Your Own Business for Entrepreneurs

- → the works manager knows that they really must get round to updating the company's health and safety policies;
- → the householder with rotten windows knows that sometime soon they must buy replacement windows;
- → the 80-year-old widower knows that keeping his house clean is becoming more of a challenge every week and that soon he must find a cleaner.

What each of these people lacks is the sense of urgency that will lead them to make their decision immediately. They know that they have a need. However, the need is not yet pressing enough for them to go out and look for a solution. What they need help with is deciding to do something about it now.

Case study
Ian Pocock, Peak Electromagnetics,
www.peak-em.co.uk

A chartered engineer, Ian Pocock, established Peak Electromagnetics in 2004. The company provides comprehensive support to manufacturers, reliably and effectively taking their products from concept through to testing.

Before starting his own business, Ian had been providing consultancy services as an employee, so he was accustomed to managing his time and projects. However, selling himself was something he'd not done before.

'Most of the information I could find was helpful for people selling products, not services,' he explained. 'I found **www.shout99.com**, a UK freelancers' online network, to be a really helpful source of practical advice.'

The sales process, step by step

When you start a sales conversation, both parties will know that you are about to talk business. That does not mean you have to start talking formally, or use different words. It means you have to take control of the conversation and gently steer it along a logical path. That logical path can be defined in the following way.

Preparation

Before you start your sales conversation, make sure you have fully prepared. This is your business now and your prospective new customer will expect you to know the answers and to be able to make decisions.

You prepare for a sales conversation by:

→ being familiar with what you are trying to sell;

→ knowing exactly what deal you can strike and still make a profit;

→ having checked out your prospect and having some idea about what might motivate them to buy (although you will not have a closed mind);

→ checking that the person you are talking to has the authority to make the purchase – for example, at home the customer will usually want to ask their partner before committing; at work the person you are talking to might have the authority to agree the specification but lack the budgetary responsibility to make the actual purchase.

Approach

Next, you need to get your prospect's attention and start a conversation. If you are meeting somebody by appointment this is not a problem. If they have walked into your shop and are looking intently at a particular product, then it can be difficult to know how to go about starting a conversation. The same is true if you are at an exhibition and somebody comes to your stand or perhaps just pauses in the aisle to read one of your displays. You can make your approach and break the ice by:

→ walking into their field of vision (rather than creeping up from behind);

→ asking what interests them about whatever it is they are looking at;

→ introducing yourself and paying them an appropriate compliment;

→ smiling.

How to Start Your Own Business for Entrepreneurs

Prepare properly before starting your sales meeting. You need to have answers to the most likely questions at your fingertips.

Exploring their needs

Once you have broken the ice and started a conversation you need to take it somewhere constructive. You do that by asking questions that will help you understand their needs and motivation. The context within which the conversation takes place will help you to start. For example, in a shop or at an exhibition, finding out how, where and why they might use whatever it is you are displaying is a natural place to go. If you are meeting them by appointment they will expect to be asked questions that relate to your products or services.

Danger!

If you ask lots of closed questions – those that demand yes or no answers – there is a risk that your questioning will appear aggressive and almost an interrogation. You overcome this by asking open and closed questions and taking the time to listen and respond to what they tell you.

In other words

Open questions usually include the words who, what, where, why and when. They encourage the other person to open up and share information.

Closed questions usually demand a short answer, often yes or no. They are used to check understanding and gain commitment.

In a sales conversation you will use open questions to learn more about the other person and what interests them. When you want to change direction or focus them on a particular aspect of what they have said you use a closed question to stop the flow and take them in the direction you want to go. Use open questions to go faster and closed questions to slow down. Vary the speed according to the route you're taking.

Presenting your solution

Having worked out the other person's needs (that you can meet), it is time to suggest your solution. You start by summarising what it is you think your prospect wants and why. Use a closed question to get them to confirm that this is the case, or to tell you more if you have not quite got it right.

Then, using a phrase such as 'Let me tell you about XYZ', you can present your solution to their need. When describing benefits you can offer, place the greatest emphasis on those most relevant to their need. In other words, put aside your own views about what is most important and concentrate instead on theirs.

In the factory we make cosmetics; in the drugstore we sell hope. CHARLES REVSON

Getting commitment

Now that you have identified your customer's need and explained why your product or service solves the problem, it is time to get commitment. It is human nature to put off making a commitment and your job is to stop that happening.

The art of getting commitment is to make it as easy as possible for the other person to say yes. You can do this by:

→ summarising the argument for purchase and then asking for the order;

→ breaking the deal down and committing them to one piece at a time, building up to a whole;

→ offering them two alternatives, both of which involve saying yes – for example, 'Would you like it delivered on Tuesday or Thursday next week?'

If you have found out enough to really understand the need and have presented your case clearly, getting commitment should happen naturally. If you meet resistance you have not done your job properly.

Overcoming objections

Inevitably, there will be some barriers to saying yes straight away. Asking for commitment is a good way to identify what the sticking points are. When your prospect says no, you need to find out why. You do this by saying something like:

→ 'Could you tell me what it is you're not yet sure about?'

→ 'From our conversation I thought you could see why this is a good move for you. What is holding you back?'

Sometimes there might be a very good reason why the person is unable to place an order at that time. When this happens you have to arrange to get back in touch when they are ready.

Once you are working through the objections and dealing with them one by one, you are at the most focused stage of the sales interview. Your conversation will cycle between dealing with objections and seeking commitment. Your goal is to gain some commitment if not the order.

Danger!

If you try too hard to get commitment (called 'closing the deal'), you risk alienating your prospect. You have to watch their body language and listen to what they say to decide when the time has come to call a halt. What is important is that you leave the meeting with some commitment, even if it is only to talk again in a month or two.

Case study

David Aldridge, Herne Bay Mobility,
www.hernebaymobility.co.uk

Redundancy from a senior management position gave David Aldridge the push he needed to start Herne Bay Mobility. Most of his customers are elderly and, as he told me, 'are not a group of people hard to sell to.' That said, he does believe in being professional. 'Selling skills are essential,' he says. 'However, if it is the right product for the customer and the quality and price are good, then 75 per cent of your job is done for you.'

Something of a computer enthusiast, David conducts much of his business online, where it is even more important to play it straight. eBay and Amazon, for example, have strict rules for traders and your reputation depends on positive customer feedback.

David is successful because he knows both how to sell and when to simply let the customers make the decision for themselves.

How to get lasting commitment

Few businesses seek to sell to each customer only once. It is far easier to get repeat business or recommendations from your existing customers than to recruit and to convert new ones. As you become established you should find that an increasing proportion of your turnover comes from repeat or introduced business. This makes life far easier and more pleasant as you are dealing with people you know.

Repeat orders and recommendations do not happen spontaneously. You have to nurture them by building a lasting and meaningful relationship with your customer. This starts the moment they agree to the first transaction.

It is important that you confirm in writing, perhaps via email, what was agreed when you closed the sale. You can use the same communication to reinforce the positive reasons why the customer has bought from you. You can also make the point that you grow your business by recommendation and would love to meet anyone your customer feels might be interested in what you have to offer.

Good ways to keep in touch and build your relationship with your customers include:

→ regular newsletters and updates that offer useful information, not just sales messages;

→ proactive customer service, including courtesy calls to check that all is well and sales calls at around the time the customer is likely to be buying more;

→ incentives to introduce new customers or to try new products/services;

→ encouraging them to sponsor various charitable activities you might engage in – for example, you might run a marathon to raise money for your local hospice.

Keeping track of your sales leads

As your business grows you will gain more and more customers. You will also find that you have an increasing number of prospects, some lukewarm and some quite hot. It can be difficult to keep track of when you have promised to get back to people and what you have been talking about.

Most people find it helpful to use what is called CRM software. CRM stands for customer relationship management. There are several on the market to choose from, none too expensive for the start-up business.

Time saver

CRM software is cheap and easy to use. It can give you the discipline you need to keep on top of your growing pool of prospects. Use it!

Frequently asked questions

Here are some typical questions that new entrepreneurs ask about sales.

We sell and lay brick-paved drives and patios. The problem we have is that although people love the product and seem happy with the price, they always want to put off doing the job until later. How can we get commitment from people to do something now?

You need to create a sense of urgency and take away some of the pain of the big invoice when the job is finished. I suspect you would also benefit from being able to schedule your work more effectively, so that you lay patios when it suits you rather than being very busy and then very quiet. You need to break the year into campaigns and then have a different incentive to purchase for each campaign. For example, you might offer spread payments so that customers can have the patio now and pay over three months. You might also offer free extras such as drain covers at certain times of the year.

I am not a salesman by any stretch of the imagination. Why can't I just hire someone to do the selling for me?

Talking to your prospective customers will teach you more about what your business needs to do to succeed than anything else. You cannot afford to delegate all your sales activity to other people unless you want to risk losing touch with what your business really does.

We have a shop and I find it really difficult to break the ice and start conversations. I find myself saying silly things like, 'Can I help you?' Can you help me?

Perhaps your shop layout makes it difficult to saunter up to people and start a conversation. Would it help if you arranged things differently? You might also try offering samples if that is appropriate, or even saying that you are conducting a survey to find out what people think of a particular product. In many ways it doesn't matter where you start, you just need to start!

If you would like to look at the sales process in more depth, see *Selling for Entrepreneurs*, one of the other titles in this series. Another key aspect of entrepreneurial success is building a great reputation. You'll discover how to do that in the next chapter.

Key points

→ Make sure the person you are speaking to has the authority to buy.

→ A sales conversation should feel natural and be enjoyed by both parties.

→ Practise following the sales sequence in this chapter and make it second nature.

→ Invest in software that will help you to keep in touch with your prospects.

→ Do not take it personally when people say no – they are rejecting the offer and not you.

Next steps

What action will you take to apply the information in this chapter? By when will you do it?

_____

_____

_____

_____

Reputation – making friends and influencing people

Good news spreads fast, particularly if you encourage it. Chapter Fifteen looked at how PR can help you build a good reputation, but what exactly is reputation and how can you influence it? In a world where products and services are all pretty much the same, your personal reputation will increasingly make all the difference.

Online marketplaces such as eBay measure reputation. People will use your reputation rating to decide whether they want to do business with you. The traders on eBay work hard to maintain a high reputation rating. These ratings are based on the speed with which you dispatch goods that have been ordered from you and how well you handle any disputes.

In the face-to-face business world, as opposed to online, reputation is more complex. However, as with the eBay reputation rating, it is what you do and how you do it that will dictate how good your reputation is in your marketplace.

You can't build a reputation on what you are going to do. HENRY FORD

What is reputation and why is it important?

When Gerald Ratner was misquoted as describing his company's products as crap, his company soon went out of business. The inference was that he was exploiting his customers by selling them cheap tat. It took him many years to live down that moment and to rebuild his entrepreneurial career.

Sir Richard Branson, on the other hand, has a consistently good reputation for challenging a marketplace, by introducing competition to reduce prices and improve the customer deal. The image of this successful entrepreneur as a man unafraid of a challenge is reinforced by some of his well-publicised adventures.

Reputation is, by definition, just an opinion. It is an opinion formed by those around you – in this context, your potential customers. Opinions are not necessarily based on actual knowledge, but more often on hearsay and anecdotal evidence.

Case study
Bláithín O'Reilly Murphy, Distinctive Weddings,
www.distinctiveweddings.ie

Bláithín O'Reilly Murphy tried lots of careers, including working as an interior designer and air hostess, before setting up as a wedding consultant in 2007. It seemed to be a service that encompassed much of what she'd most enjoyed doing up until then. Most of all, she wanted the freedom of being her own boss.

Much of her work comes by word of mouth, so reputation is vital. A wedding magazine editor suggested she write a book. *Distinctive Weddings – Tying the Knot without the Rope Burns!* was published in 2008, and she tells me she is 'the first Irish wedding planner to have written [a book] for the Irish market'. She is now approached whenever journalists want a comment on weddings. She is also in talks with a production company about a possible TV show.

By building her reputation in this way, her popularity as a wedding consultant has grown and her business future assured.

How to build and maintain your reputation

The best way to build your business reputation is to exceed people's expectations. However, you also have to do this without exceeding your own budget. You have to be able both to wow people and to be profitable.

Here are some simple ways a business can build its reputation:

→ Answering the phone quickly and responding to all enquiries promptly.

→ Always being helpful, polite and knowledgeable.

→ Setting and beating realistic deadlines. In other words, if you expect to deliver the goods on Wednesday, promise delivery on Thursday to give yourself some leeway. Then, when you deliver on Wednesday, you look very efficient.

→ Being more than fair when dealing with product returns or customer complaints. It is often better to bend to meet the demands of the slightly unrealistic complainant than to suffer the consequences of them bad-mouthing you all around the neighbourhood.

→ Associating yourself and your business with worthwhile causes and projects. Be careful not to let these take over your life, but giving a small part of your profits to a local charity will work wonders for your business reputation (and probably give you a better return on investment than some other forms of marketing).

In a world where the internet can reveal some of the most intimate details of our personal lives to anyone caring to look, reputations built at work can be shattered at home. Of course, you cannot realistically live every moment as if your business depended upon it, but you can consider the potential business consequences before, for example, having a rant at a local shopkeeper who has wound you up on a Saturday afternoon.

How your reputation can work for you

A good reputation does much more for your business than simply win you more customers. Reputation can be reflected in the value of your business, listed on the balance sheet as 'goodwill' (see next section).

Another word for reputation is popularity. When you are popular people want to be with you. In a business context this may be reflected in the following ways:

→ People will like doing business with you. This means greater customer loyalty and customers who will tell you if you need to change your offer to stay in the market.

→ Suppliers will want to help you succeed. This means getting supplied ahead of less popular rivals in times of scarcity and perhaps even some leniency if you need longer to pay now and again.

→ Employees will be more enthusiastic and less likely to leave. Your workforce will also be willing to do that little bit extra because they will have bought into your vision for the business.

→ Neighbours will be more tolerant. For example, if they are frequently asked to sign for deliveries when you are out, or if at times your business makes a lot of noise or takes up a lot of parking at a business centre.

Case study
Gavin Peck, Verbatim Call Centres,
www.thephoneansweringservice.co.uk

Gavin Peck and Graham Hill set up Verbatim in 1997. Both had previously enjoyed successful international careers. They had been publishing directories together and found small businesses very bad at answering the phone. This sparked the idea.

However, they were competing with huge call centres that pen poorly trained and seldom motivated staff in what Gavin calls 'coops'. He and Graham decided to be different. They wanted to offer a really personal and professional call-answering service.

Today the business is thriving. Staff are carefully selected, trained and motivated. Average length of service is five years. Customers range from huge public sector organisations to one-man bands. Like the team who handle their calls, they tend to stay for many years.

The business has a great reputation and a healthy bottom line.

Reputation and your business's value

When you look at a large company's balance sheet you will sometimes see a value attributed to 'goodwill'. Goodwill is used to describe reputation in monetary terms.

Building goodwill can be very important if you want to sell your business at some time in the future. For example, take two identical window cleaning companies. Both employ five people and both have annual sales of £300,000. The owners both want to sell their businesses at the same time.

Here are some facts about business A:

→ It has a reputation for cutting corners and skimping on jobs when under pressure.
→ The workforce do not take pride in their work and there had been complaints that they loiter and smoke outside customers' premises.
→ The workforce are paid little above minimum wage and enjoy a few work benefits.
→ By keeping overheads very low, business is more profitable.

Here are some facts about business B:

→ It gives its regular customers flowers at Christmas and always phones to check whether it is convenient before arriving to clean windows.
→ It takes staff off the road one day a month for customer care training and teambuilding days.
→ It pays its workforce a fair basic wage plus bonuses when they achieve productivity targets.
→ It is less profitable than business A.

When the owners started to market their businesses, potential buyers understandably wanted reassurance that the customers would remain loyal to the new firm, as would the workforce. They wanted things to continue very much as before and would be relying on the goodwill of the customer base to maintain the business and generate the income needed to buy out the existing owners.

If you were buying one of these two businesses, which would you choose?

In my mind there is no doubt that you would buy business B and set out to poach customers from business A as the easy way to grow the business further.

 You earn reputation by trying to do hard things well. JEFF BEZOS

Frequently asked questions

Here are some questions that new entrepreneurs have asked in regard to reputation.

I started my business after leaving prison and coming off drugs. How can I possibly build a good reputation when people know about my past?
It is the fact that you have changed your life in such a dramatic way that will make you popular and build your reputation. We cannot change the past but we can certainly change the future. Many in your situation would have taken the easier path and not started a business. People will respect you for that.

We provide domiciliary care services to the elderly and, whatever we do to please them, they are by their very nature grumpy and unappreciative at times. I think we go well beyond what is expected but I don't think this group of customers realises that. How can we build our reputation?
I would argue that the people you need to influence in terms of reputation are not the elderly themselves, but their friends and family who, but for you, would be the ones caring for them. Why not start sending regular updates and information to the next of kin of those you care for? It is these people who will be recommending you to others with aged parents needing care.

I have no intention of ever selling my business, so adding value in terms of goodwill does not appeal as much as making a bigger profit right now. Am I wrong?
I would say that you are not wrong but short-sighted. Just suppose you want to borrow money in the future. Would your bank not prefer to lend to someone with a great reputation, rather than to a business that milks every opportunity for as much as it can get?

Another aspect of starting a business that some entrepreneurs find daunting is handling finances. In the next chapter you'll discover how to make the process relatively painless.

Key points

You build a good reputation by:

→ being firm but fair;

→ exceeding expectations;

→ playing an active role in the wider world;

→ being honest;

→ being profitable so that you can continue to build your reputation.

Next steps

What action will you take to apply the information in this chapter? By when will you do it?

_____

_____

_____

_____

Managing
your business

Part Four

How to do your book-keeping without tears

Chapter Nineteen

You can look upon keeping the books as a chore – or you can learn how keeping your finger on your business's pulse can be both enjoyable and informative.

Many people use a freelance book-keeper to do their basic book-keeping, calculate VAT returns and prepare the monthly payroll.

Others prefer to do these tasks themselves, recognising that it is not difficult to keep the books straight in a relatively uncomplicated start-up business. You may surprise yourself when you find out how little time it can take to do the paperwork if you start out with a good, simple system.

> ## In this world nothing can be said to be certain, except death and taxes. BENJAMIN FRANKLIN

Why is book-keeping so important?

There is no law that says you have to keep any records at all, unless you are trading as a limited company or registered charity, in which case you are legally bound to prepare accounts. Most business start-ups are either sole traders or partnerships and as such their annual tax bill is calculated from their annual tax return.

To complete your tax return you need accurate records of your income and expenditure. You must be able to back up your tax return with documentary evidence should the tax authorities want to check. Therefore, it makes sense to keep comprehensive records of your business transactions and to keep these totally separate from your personal finances.

If you have previously been employed, you will be familiar with having your tax and National Insurance deducted from your pay before you receive it. Now that you have your own business, you will pay a flat rate of National Insurance and your income tax twice a year, in January and July. Your employer will have been responsible for calculating these deductions. Now that you are your own employer it is your responsibility. That is another good reason for keeping accurate accounts.

If you have always been employed, you may not have been asked to complete a tax return. Because, as an entrepreneur, your income and

How to Start Your Own Business for Entrepreneurs

expenditure are more complex, HM Revenue & Customs (HMRC) give you a tax return on which to provide them with the details they need. Most people complete their tax returns online.

What do you do first?

When you decide to start your own business it is important to take as much advice as possible. Remember that the tax authorities are there to help you get things right, as well as to collect tax from you.

Here are some important first steps to take when you start your business:

→ Contact HMRC (**www.hmrc.gov.uk**), the UK government department that deals with personal tax and National Insurance. Use your latest tax office reference number to locate the right office and let them know that you are starting your own business. Their website has some useful downloads and they can offer advice.

→ If you expect your turnover to exceed £65,000 in the first year you might choose to register for VAT straight away. This is handled by a separate department within HMRC. Again, their website contains a lot of useful information. Note that you do not have to register until the quarter after your turnover exceeds the registration threshold.

→ Contact your insurance broker if you are going to be using your car for business purposes or if you are going to work from home. There is a risk that if you do not inform your insurance company and have a claim relating to your business activities they might refuse to pay out. You will also need public liability insurance, which is very cheap to obtain, but let your broker advise you.

→ Open a business bank account. Most banks have new business starter packs and offer at least 12 months' free banking. Don't automatically go to the bank you use personally; often it is a good idea to keep your business and personal finances completely separate.

What records should you keep?

Your business bank statements and a written record (supported by invoices and receipts) of each transaction is essentially all you need to have. When the time comes to submit your tax return you will need this information to complete the form.

You also need to keep a record of any other expenses that you have incurred in the course of your business that can be allowed against your trading income. These may not all be transactions made through a business account because some of your domestic bills may be allowable. For example, if you are self-employed or in a partnership and work from home you may be able to claim:

→ a proportion of your home heating and electricity bills;

→ some of your mortgage interest;

→ your broadband subscription;

→ other expenses directly linked to your business.

In addition, if you use your car for work, you can offset most of the running costs and depreciation within certain limits.

Danger!

It can be tempting to try to claim much more than you really should. However, if you're using 10 per cent of your home as an office, for example, then claiming 10 per cent of household bills seems reasonable and is unlikely to be challenged.

 My money goes to my agent, then to my accountant and from him to the tax man.

GLENDA JACKSON

Simple systems to make life easier

With more than 300,000 people starting a business in the UK every year, it is not surprising that there are some very efficient book-keeping software packages on the market. They are affordable and some can be upgraded to more sophisticated versions as your business grows.

Some, such as Sage Instant (**www.shop.sage.co.uk**), Quickbooks (**www. QuickBooks.co.uk**), and Cashflow Manager (**www.cashflow-manager.com/uk**), come on a CD with a handbook to get you started. Others such as Kashflow (**www.kashflow.co.uk**), are web-based and you pay a monthly subscription.

If you are using an accountant to prepare annual accounts and complete your tax returns (which usually proves to be a sound investment), use a software package they recommend. You can then simply email them your accounts as an attachment and they can open it at their end to check.

Danger!

Don't complicate a simple business by using a more sophisticated accounting package than you need. Start simple and upgrade later.

Understanding the jargon

When you are new to entrepreneurship, the terminology and jargon used by accountants and bank managers can seem daunting. Here are some of the words you will encounter, explained in everyday language:

Assets: physical things your business owns that have a financial value.

Liabilities: the general term embracing all things your business owes.

Long-term liabilities: usually debts that are not yet due for repayment in total – for example, mortgages and business loans.

Short-term liabilities: the things you have to pay for soon.

Debtors: the term used to describe people who owe you money – in other words, customers who have been invoiced for completed work.

Creditors: the people who have invoiced you for the things you have bought.

Balance sheet: literally balances your assets and liabilities and calculates the net value of your business. On one side it totals your physical assets and debtors and on the other your total liabilities including creditors. The balance sheet will show long-term liabilities separately because, although they affect the value of the business, they are not due for payment yet and will contribute to future income.

Profit and loss account: this year's trading performance over a period of time, arrived at by comparing your income with your payments. As your business grows you will find it useful to prepare a monthly profit and loss account so that you can see that everything is on track.

Income and expenditure: income from sales and costs incurred.

Cash flow: the flow of money in and out of your business. Sometimes people talk about a positive cash flow; this is where you receive payment for something before you have had to pay your suppliers. For example, a fish and chip shop will pay for its potatoes a month after delivery. People buying fish and chips pay straight away, so you have been paid for the potatoes before you have to pay for them.

Gross margin: your selling price less the costs directly attributable to that sale, such as materials.

Overheads: business costs that cannot directly be attributed to a specific sale – for example, labour, rent and finance costs.

Bottom line: your net profit.

Finding time

Doing the books need not be an arduous task. Once you have set up your accounting software with headings that suit your business, it should take you no more than a couple of hours a month to keep your books up to date.

It is always good practice to complete your book-keeping soon after the end of each month. This will give you a good feel for how your business is doing and enable you to spot any errors you might have missed during the month.

If you have a book-keeping system that does not record each invoice as it is raised, but rather when it is paid, you also need to make time to check through your file of unpaid invoices so that any now-overdue payments can be chased up.

Time saver

Find time to do the books at the start of each month. You'll then quickly spot any mistakes/mis-payments made in the previous month and it will take less time than if you let the paperwork pile up.

How to choose the right accountant

Choosing an accountant is like buying shoes for a child. You are looking for a comfortable fit and also room for growth. However, buy shoes that are too large or too small and they will be uncomfortable to wear and possibly damage your feet.

Accountants, like shoes, come in many shapes and sizes. An accountancy practice that works with major corporations is unlikely to be the right one for a start-up business, unless that start-up business is going to become a major corporation quickly.

The best accountants win new clients by recommendation. You can shortcut this process by asking people you know and respect whether they would recommend their accountant to you. Like doctors, accountants are very strict about client confidentiality and will never discuss your business with another client. Look for an accountant who:

→ you can relate to as a person;
→ understands your business sector;
→ is enthusiastic about your new enterprise;
→ has recognised accountancy qualifications;
→ appreciates that as a start-up you have a limited budget.

Danger!

As with any professional adviser, do not necessarily go with the first accountant you meet. It is quite usual for people to meet two or three accountants before making their choice.

Frequently asked questions

The following are some typical questions that new entrepreneurs have about book-keeping and accountants.

I started my business last year and was shocked at the size of my accountant's invoice when she prepared my first year's accounts. I had done my own book-keeping but the bill was still larger than I had expected. Is this normal?

There are two things to comment on here. First, it will always cost more for your accountant to deal with your first year's trading as you both are doing things for the first time. Ask for an estimate of next year's costs so that you do not get an unpleasant surprise. Second, many accountants are happy for clients to pay their fee by instalments throughout the year. This helps their cash flow as well as yours.

I have found an accountant I would like to use and they have suggested doing everything for me, including preparing management accounts. All I have to do is drop in the copy invoices and bills every month and they will do the rest. This sounds good – what do you think?

How to Start Your Own Business for Entrepreneurs

I think this sounds expensive and, unless you are completely daunted by the prospect of doing any of it yourself, I would advise against outsourcing everything. As your business grows, you will spot things while doing your monthly accounts that the professionals might miss.

A friend I play golf with tells me that he takes most of his income from his business as dividends. What does this mean and should I be doing the same?
When you have a limited liability company (Ltd), the profits can be distributed to the shareholders as dividends. These are taxed differently from the salary your friend will be taking through the year. In some situations, accountants advise clients with limited companies to take most of their income as dividends, as this can mean a lower tax bill.

When you are keeping current with your accounts, you will always know how large your profits are. Of course, you will always want them to be larger – and that is the topic of the next chapter.

Key points

→ Tell the tax authorities when you are starting your business and seek their help in getting things organised.
→ Keep your business and personal finances completely separate.
→ Find a good accountant to deal with your tax affairs.

Next steps

What action will you take to apply the information in this chapter? By when will you do it?

_____

_____

_____

_____

↑

How to make your profits bigger

Chapter Twenty

A popular adage used by business advisers is to say that 'turnover is vanity and profit is sanity'. The saying is popular because, too often, people starting and growing a business focus on increasing their sales turnover without paying due regard to profitability.

Of course, you need a level of turnover to cover your overhead costs, but in nine out of ten businesses, the best way to make more money is to improve the profitability, not increase the turnover. This is because more sales mean more production, which means more overheads and more costs. If you can increase the profitability of your existing turnover, nothing changes apart from the bottom line.

Naturally, your customers will not simply volunteer to give you a greater margin on the business you do together. You cannot just reduce the specification and quality of what you do and expect to retain the same price. This will not please your customers. Instead, you have to add value so that your customers are happy to do business with you and willingly pay a premium price for a premium service.

If you mean to profit, learn to please.

WINSTON CHURCHILL

What is the difference between turnover and profit?

Imagine for a moment that you run a boarding kennels. People leave their dogs with you when they go away on holiday or are unable temporarily to care for their pet at home. You charge your customers on a per dog per day basis.

The amount of food a dog eats, not surprisingly, depends on its size. A big dog will eat three times as much food as a small dog. Both dogs occupy the same space and take the same amount of time to look after. So, the more small dogs you have in your kennels, the more profitable your business is because you are buying less food – as the following illustration shows.

Twenty dogs 'paying' £50 per week gives you a weekly turnover of £1,000. Your average weekly costs are as follows:

How to Start Your Own Business for Entrepreneurs

Labour	£500
Materials	£100
Food	£200
Total	**£800**

Therefore, your profit is £1,000 – £800 = £200, or 20 per cent of turnover.

Now, you have noticed that when you have a lot of large dogs, your food bill goes up to £250 a week. If you have a lot of small dogs it drops to £150 a week. In other words, if you have a lot of large dogs your weekly profit can fall to £150 and if you have a lot of small dogs it can rise to £250. Multiply this by 50 weeks in the year (as you'll need some holiday) and the potential additional profit from housing only small dogs is £5,000.

The way to make more profit from the same turnover with this business is to specialise in catering for the needs of small dogs. You might find that owners of small dogs are different from owners of large dogs, so you might focus your marketing on meeting the needs of the small-dog owner.

To look at this another way, you would need to extend your kennels to accommodate more dogs and possibly hire in more labour if you wanted to make the same additional profit by catering for large dogs. Focusing on increasing profit rather than turnover dramatically reduces your need for investment and the risk associated with seeking additional customers.

Now look and see how you can apply the same principle to your business.

Why will some deals always make more than others?

Some deals will always make more money than others. For one thing, when you first start your business you will almost inevitably be so enthusiastic to get some sales that you will do deals that in the future you would not consider worthwhile. The challenge there is to move away from those unprofitable customers as soon as you can.

As a rule of thumb, the more value you add to your customer's life or business, the more they will pay for what you do. For example, a graphic designer creating a full-page advertisement will be able to charge a higher fee to a large company placing this in a national publication than to a small company placing a similar ad in a local newspaper. This is because the ad in the national publication has potential to make much more money for the advertiser. Both adverts probably took the same amount of time and effort to create.

The more value you add, the more the customer will pay. Value is different from cost! Generally, you will be able to make higher profits from deals that are done with the following customers:

→ Larger customers with the potential to place bigger orders. They often take less time to make up their mind than people placing small orders.

→ People who themselves run successful organisations or have high personal income. They will be able to work out the return they will get on their investment in your business.

→ Organisations where the positive impact of your work can be large. These will also be quicker decision makers than people for whom the purchase is not crucial to their short-term success.

→ People with a problem that needs fixing quickly. For example, repairs on oil rigs where every hour of lost production means a huge financial loss to the rig operator.

Generally, you will make smaller profits from deals that are done with the following customers:

→ People with limited budgets who have to make every penny count.

→ Individuals who do not value their own time and will be unlikely to value yours.

→ Organisations where the benefit you can deliver is marginal.

→ People with problems that will only slowly get worse. For example, persuading a restaurant owner to replace worn flooring will not be easy until it becomes dangerous. The disruption of replacing it will encourage the restaurateur to put off repair as long as possible.

Danger!

The 80/20 rule applies here as much as anywhere else. Twenty per cent of your customers will give you 80 per cent of your profit. Do not allow yourself to be distracted by the 80 per cent of your customers who together only give you 20 per cent of your profit. Always focus on the most lucrative customers.

Danger

> # The successful man will profit from his mistakes and try again in a different way. DALE CARNEGIE

How to work out your profitability

You will only know which of your transactions are the most profitable if you measure your profitability deal by deal. This is easy if you are selling your time as a self-employed consultant. Your costs will remain largely the same irrespective of the daily fee you charge your client. Therefore the higher the day rate you charge, the more profitable the client becomes for you.

If you make or sell products, your profitability can be harder to work out. You have to produce enough sales to cover your overhead costs. For instance, if you have an ice cream van and park beside the beach, you must sell enough ice cream to cover the cost of the van before you make any money for yourself. You might calculate your profitability like this:

Ice cream van cost you £10,000 and will last five years	£2,000 pa
Running costs, fuel, repairs and insurance	£2,000 pa
Total running costs	**£4,000 pa**
Trading days (summer and weekends)	200
Income needed to cover overheads	£200/day

You buy ice creams for £1 each and sell them for £2. You have to sell 200 ice creams a day to cover your overheads and reach breakeven point. After you have sold your first 200 ice creams, you know that you are making £1 per ice cream for yourself.

However, if you are the only ice cream van on the beach and the weather is hot, you can sell at a higher price as people are otherwise faced with a long walk. This means you need to sell less to cover your daily overheads and start making money sooner.

The key to calculating your profitability is knowing:

→ what your overhead costs are;

→ what your buying price is for products and raw materials;

→ what costs are incurred in processing, in preparing and packing (as these can be easily overlooked);

→ what the market price is so that you are not selling too cheaply.

Time saver

Big customers are often easier to sell to and more rational than small ones. Focus on winning big customers.

Case study

Jonny White, Zimma Web Development, www.zimma.co.uk

By the time Jonny White graduated with a software engineering degree, he had already established a thriving business building and maintaining websites. He enjoyed the work and charged what seemed like a lot of money at the time: £9 per hour.

As his workload grew he realised he could not afford to take on staff and continue to make a profit. He had to either increase his prices or turn work away.

His customers had also been telling him he was too cheap, so when Jonny increased his prices, he kept most of his customers and was able to employ an assistant. His business began to grow. He also now has time to set aside to plan his future. As he said to me, 'I now feel I'm running my business rather than my business running me.'

How to Start Your Own Business for Entrepreneurs

How to add extra profit without really trying

There are two ways to add additional profit to each deal that you do. The first is to reduce your costs and the second is to increase your margin.

Cutting costs

There are two aspects to this. The first is to keep your overhead costs as low as possible. Your overhead costs have to be covered by all of your sales in the year. For example, you might:

→ shop around to save money on things like insurance and not simply renew each year without checking;

→ make your business as green as possible so that your energy consumption is low;

→ hire in specialist equipment only when you need it, rather than buy or lease it and have it as an overhead cost.

You can reduce the costs associated directly with delivering your products and services (these are called variable costs) in many ways. For example, you might:

→ pay less for raw materials;

→ increase your efficiency;

→ buy stock and raw materials only when you need them so that you are not financing stock;

→ contract out your delivery rather than running your own van.

Increasing margin

There is often more scope to increase your profit by making a greater margin on each sale that you make. Here are some examples.

→ Charge for things that you might otherwise give away for free.
   — Why not charge for delivery?
   __ Why not charge to take away and recycle the machine you are replacing?

— Why not agree an ongoing monthly fee to cover maintenance rather than waiting for the client to call you when things break down?

→ Sell extras – in particular, other things that you know your customer will need. Here are some examples.
— A garage offers to valet cars when in for a service at a discount from the usual rate.
— An off-licence sells or hires glasses.
— A carpet cleaning contractor offers to organise curtain cleaning as well and subcontracts the work to a local laundry.

Make a list of the other things that your customers will buy at the same time as they are buying from you. Work out how you can supply those, too, making life easier for your customers and more profitable for yourself.

Time

One of the biggest pitfalls into which new entrepreneurs tumble is to overlook the cost of their own time. If you are engrossed in what you are doing it is very easy to forget how much time something is taking. If you have started your own business, you will be working long hours – and all of these should be paid for by your customers.

Managing your time, and in particular recording it, is one of the most important things you can do when you start a business. You can buy simple software packages that sit on your PC and will log your time against different jobs. Easier, perhaps, is just to write down in your diary each day how many hours you spend on each job. You will be surprised at how much time you are not charging for or are building into the cost of the products or services you are delivering.

Danger!

If you are selling your time, either as a consultant or delivering a service, assume that you will sell only three days per week of your time. The rest will be taken up by administration, marketing, cancellations and 'stuff'. 'Stuff' is an all-embracing term to cover those things you did not plan to do but found you had to do anyway!

Frequently asked questions

The following are some questions that entrepreneurs have asked about how to increase profits.

It's all very well saying sell to bigger customers, but I have a retail shop in a fairly hard-up town. How can I go upmarket and make more money?

I guess one thing you could do is to market yourself to more affluent people living a little further away. The appeal to them could be that you are cheaper than the more trendy outlets they are accustomed to shopping in. The other option is to look for more and more budget brands that you can sell at an affordable price and still make a decent margin.

We are running a social enterprise and want to make a difference, not a profit. What does all this mean to us?

Please do not think that a social enterprise is not about profit. What sets you apart from the for-profit business is that you are choosing to invest your profits in helping people over some particular disadvantage. Everything here about increasing your profit applies equally to a social enterprise.

We are a wholesale tree grower. Our customers are garden centres. How can we add value? I'm struggling to see the opportunity for us.

Every business has the opportunity to add value and increase its margins in some way. One obvious opportunity is to develop a retail brand and sell direct to people with large gardens via the internet. They will pay for delivery and you would save the garden centre's margin. You might use a different trading name for this so that you do not end up competing with your garden centre customers.

While it will be very satisfying to watch your business grow, that growth brings with it some additional things to watch for, as you'll discover in the next chapter.

Key points

→ It takes no longer to win a large order than it does to win a small one.

→ The more difference your product or service makes, the higher your profit from that transaction can and should be.

→ Reducing your costs can increase your profits by more than increasing your price.

→ Do not overlook the time it takes you to do what you do. Your time has to be paid for somehow.

Next steps

What action will you take to apply the information in this chapter? By when will you do it?

_____

_____

_____

_____

↑

Financial factors to watch as you start to grow

Chapter Twenty-one

Watching your business grow and evolve will be one of the most satisfying things you do over the coming years. What right now might be little more than an idea on a piece of paper will develop into a thriving enterprise, perhaps even a household name.

You have already read about the importance of accurate book-keeping and also some ways to make your profits bigger. Now it is time to take a closer look at some of the financial implications of business growth.

It is a fact that more businesses fail when they are growing than when they are shrinking. This is because they simply run out of money. However, growing your business is something you do not want to avoid, because standing still really is not an option.

This chapter will help you ride the wave of business growth.

 **Be not afraid of growing slowly; be afraid only of standing still.** CHINESE PROVERB

Why every business should seek growth

Nothing in life or business ever stays the same. In many ways a business is like a person. It is born, grows, matures, ages and then moves on in some way. The serial entrepreneur will grow a business to the point at which they think they will achieve the best sale price and then they sell. Others keep their business to the point beyond which it has value and are forced to close it down.

Whatever your ambition for your business, it will evolve and grow because you will constantly need new customers to replace those that fall away. Both you and your new customers will have different expectations, as you will be more experienced and they will be buying from a more established business.

What you can do and indeed should do is to manage the rate of growth to keep business evolving in line with your own ambition.

You will either step forward into growth or you will step back into safety. ABRAHAM MASLOW

How to Start Your Own Business for Entrepreneurs

What is solvency and how does it change?

A business is solvent when it can pay its current business debts as they become due. It is insolvent if it cannot pay its debts or if the assets of the business are less than the debts.

As a business grows, often there is a lag between the growth in costs and the increased income resulting from those costs. In other words, even though you have lots of orders, you have to buy the materials and hire people to fulfil those orders before seeing the income from this additional work. If you have to pay for supplies before you see the income from customers your cash flow is squeezed. This is sometimes called 'overtrading'.

An example would be a company that buys timber and sells shelves to a DIY store which then sells them on to the general public. The timber supplier demands payment within 30 days of supply and the DIY store pays the company at the end of the month following supply.

The wholesale price for which the company sells its shelves to the DIY store is exactly twice the price it pays for its timber. In other words, it takes £500 worth of timber to make £1,000 worth of shelves.

The shelves are proving popular and orders are growing. The DIY store orders ahead like this:

	Month 1	Month 2	Month 3	Month 4
Orders placed	£1,000	£2,000	£4,000	£6,000

And here is the impact on the books of the company that makes the shelves:

	Month 1	Month 2	Month 3	Month 4
Opening bank balance	£500	£0	£0	£0
Purchases	£500	£1,000	£2,000	£3,000
Income	£0	£1,000	£2,000	£4,000
Closing bank balance	£0	£0	£0	£500

You can see that even though orders are growing healthily, the company runs out of money very quickly. In this example, that would not be a problem if the company had agreed an overdraft with its bank.

Often this cash flow gap is exacerbated by the need to hire additional staff or buy more or bigger equipment. These add to the costs and inevitably have to be paid for at least in part before the sales revenue starts to build.

Danger!

Do not commit yourself to significant additional fixed costs, particularly permanent labour, until you are confident that sales growth is sustainable. If you are experiencing a temporary increase in demand, hire in the equipment you need and use agency staff.

How to manage this aspect of growth

The big issue here is that you do not necessarily have the money to cover your growing costs until your customers pay you. You can manage this funding gap by:

→ negotiating longer payment terms with your suppliers;

→ persuading your customers to pay you faster (perhaps offering a small discount for paying early);

→ forecasting your cash flow and obtaining an overdraft from your bank to fund the gap;

→ increasing your prices to keep a greater margin and perhaps limit growth resulting from you being too cheap;

→ finding an investor in your business (see Chapter Eight).

Paying late and getting paid early is a good way to boost your working capital. Only do this by negotiation though!

Case study
Don Cooke, CAL, www.teamr-cal.co.uk

Don Cooke and business partner Andrew Harris relaunched CAL as a provider of 'solutions for distributed teams' in 2004. Both were established in the IT industry and so winning and satisfying clients was not their biggest challenge.

Developing software can be expensive and there's often a time lag between creating the solution and selling it to enough customers to recoup the cost.

Don reckons they wasted money in their search for investors, although now they have the funding they need. 'How well you survive without funding is as important as how you set about seeking funding,' he commented. 'Most start-ups run out of money and usually this is ahead of securing sufficient revenue. It is persistence when that situation occurs that makes the difference between survival and failure of any business.'

What will your bank manager look out for and why?

Your bank manager will be keeping an eye on the transactions going through your account. The banks have software that uses your bank statement to analyse your business performance. These systems will alert your bank manager to any growing problem.

You must also keep an eye on some key financial ratios within your business as they can give you early warning of any looming challenge. These include the following.

Acid test

Acid test is a ratio that shows whether a company is able to pay its debts. This is the equation:

$$\text{Acid test} = \frac{\text{current assets} - \text{stock}}{\text{current liabilities}}$$

A score of greater than one passes the test. In fact, the higher the number, the better. Less than one and you are probably insolvent.

Debtor days

Debtor days is a ratio that tells you how many days on average your debtors (people who owe you money) are taking to pay. This is the equation:

$$\text{Debtor days} = \frac{\text{trade debtors}}{\text{annual sales}} \times 365$$

The lower the number the better.

Creditor days

Creditor days is a ratio that tells you how many days on average you are taking to pay your trade creditors (people to whom you owe money). This is the equation:

$$\text{Creditor days} = \frac{\text{trade creditors}}{\text{annual purchases}} \times 365$$

The equations in action

Here's an example to help you fully understand these equations. Management accounts show that, today, your company:

→ is owed £15,000;
→ owes £2,500 to suppliers, £2,000 in wages at the end of the month and £1,000 rent and rates;
→ has stock in the warehouse that cost £3,000;
→ spends £25,000 a year with suppliers;
→ has annual sales of £100,000;
→ has £2,000 in the bank.

Using these figures, we come up with the following results.

$$\text{Acid test} = \frac{\text{current assets} - \text{stock}}{\text{current liabilities}} = \frac{(£15,000 + £2,000) - £3,000}{£2,500 + £2,000 + £1,000} = 2.5$$

The company is very healthy and able to meet its commitments.

$$\text{Debtor days} = \frac{\text{trade debtors}}{\text{annual sales}} \times 365 = \frac{£15,000}{£100,000} \times 365 = 54.75 \text{ days}$$

The company's customers on average pay their invoices in 54.75 days.

$$\text{Creditor days} = \frac{\text{trade creditors}}{\text{annual purchases}} \times 365 = \frac{£2,500}{£25,000} \times 365 = 36.5 \text{ days}$$

The company on average pays its suppliers in 36.5 days.

This company is clearly in good health financially.

Danger

You can create a feeling of false security by delaying payment to your creditors. You still have money in the bank but, alas, it is not all yours!

Danger

When are these things most important?

It is always important to keep an eye on some of these key financial ratios, but more so when your business is growing rapidly. Paradoxically, it is when you are growing fast that you are at greatest risk of running out of money. This is also a period when you have very little spare time and it is easy to overlook financial management.

Other financial things to keep an eye on

There are a number of other financial indicators that it is good to monitor. Some relate to your business and others relate to your customers and even competitors. Your own performance is of paramount importance to you, but this often means more when compared with the performance of others.

The following list is not exhaustive, so use it to stimulate your thinking and build your own list. Remember that it is better to start by measuring too many things and then relax than to do it the other way round.

→ **Bank balance**. If you manage your cash flow well and have a sound business, your bank balance could at times be substantial. Most banks offering business banking will help you to set up a deposit account into which you can easily switch cash that is not needed immediately. Not only will this earn a modest rate of interest, but also it will help you discipline yourself to put money aside for tax and VAT.

→ **Credit limits**. If you use a sophisticated book-keeping package, it will allow you to set credit limits for customers and warn you if you exceed them. Your credit cards have credit limits that prevent you from borrowing more than the card company feels appropriate – you should do the same with your customers.

→ **Overdue debtors**. The simplest way to keep track of this is to file copies of invoices raised in date order, with the oldest at the front. Every week, go through the file and chase for payment those that are overdue. Make notes on the copy invoices to remind you of progress.

→ **Competitor accounts**. If your rivals are limited companies, they must file accounts with Companies House. There are a number of online databases you can subscribe to, as well as being able to order copies of their accounts from Companies House. These will help you see how your rivals are prospering (you can download any registered charity's most recent accounts free of charge from the Charity Commission website). However, if a limited company is below a certain turnover threshold, you will not be able to find their turnover and profit figures. Only companies above a certain size have to make full accounts public.

Frequently asked questions

Here are some questions that new entrepreneurs have raised regarding financial matters and business growth.

I'm semi-retired, have a pension and only want my business to pay for extras and keep my mind active. Why would I want to seek growth?
It is a fact of life that if a business is not growing, it's probably slipping behind. Growth, however, is relative to personal aspiration. Imagine yourself in a canoe,

paddling upstream in a river. If you like the view where you are, you only need to paddle hard enough to maintain your current position.

I've checked my debtor days and now realise why I'm always feeling hard up. People are taking ages to pay me! What can I do to get the money in sooner?
Here are five ways to get paid faster.

1 Take deposits and money up front from customers.
2 Invoice for payment in 14 rather than 28 days. It'll seem overdue sooner.
3 Make a courtesy call to your customer when the invoice is due, to check that all is well and that the invoice is in the next payment run.
4 Don't be embarrassed to ask for the money if it's late.
5 Take payment by instalments if your customer appears hard up and is waiting until they can pay the bill in full.

As a very small new business, it seems pretentious to set credit limits for my customers. What will they think?
In short, they needn't know. Credit limits are no more than your way of making sure you don't get too exposed to the risk of bad debt with one customer. You don't tell the customer there's a limit; you just tell them you're owed too much to continue supplying and 'need a cheque now please' if they go over the limit.

If you want to delve even more deeply into growing your business, see *How to Grow Your Business for Entrepreneurs*, one of the other titles in this series. Naturally, starting and growing a business entails some risk. In the next chapter you'll learn how to minimise risk and increase your chances of success.

Key points

→ Every business needs to grow, even to stand still.
→ Watch the key financial ratios.
→ Set credit limits for regular customers to minimise your risk.
→ If you think you're becoming insolvent, seek professional help. Often if you act quickly enough, the decline can be reversed.

Next steps

What action will you take to apply the information in this chapter? By when will you do it?

_____

_____

_____

_____

How to minimise risk and sleep well at night

Nothing we do in life is without risk. Today, more than ever before, we are all being made aware of the risks we face by organisations promoting things as diverse as healthy eating and safe driving. When you start a business you add another dimension of risk to your life.

This is because, as an entrepreneur, you are suddenly taking responsibility for things that in the past would have been taken care of by somebody else. In the early days of most businesses there is nobody else. You alone make the decisions and you alone carry the can if things go wrong.

The skill of managing risk is to keep it in perspective. The media will always remind you that at times people encounter the most horrific disasters and calamities. The majority of people start and grow their business without ever experiencing any major problems. That's because they take care to manage and thus minimise the risk to themselves, those around them and perhaps, most importantly, their livelihood.

 Every business and every product has risks. You can't get around it. LEE IACOCCA

What risks do you face when you start a business?

The most obvious risk you face when you start a business is financial. You are risking your money and perhaps also that of family and friends. You can manage financial risk by following the advice contained in the earlier chapters of this book. Working to a business plan, monitoring your financial performance and making sure you are paid on time will minimise the risk of financial disaster.

However, there are many other risks you need to be aware of.

Your health

Starting a business can be physically exhausting; however carefully you plan, you will find yourself working long hours. It is also very difficult to take time off sick. And when you are leading a very small team, it is far harder to take the odd week off, as you may have done in a former life.

If you have started your business specifically to trade life in the office for working outdoors, your health may dramatically improve. For others who find themselves compelled to work long hours with few breaks, health might suffer. To look after your health as you develop your business:

→ make sure you take time out for meals and eat sensibly;

→ find time in your life for exercise, even if it is just walking the dog every morning before you start work.

Your peace of mind

We all fear the unknown – and starting a business for the first time can be frightening. It is not unusual for new business owners to worry about their enterprise. Indeed, some anxiety is good because it focuses the mind and spurs us on. Too much stress, however, can be damaging. For your own peace of mind as you develop your new business, think about:

→ regular reality checks, comparing business performance against business goals, to help you keep things in perspective;

→ maintaining balance in your life so that your business does not occupy every waking moment.

Your relationships

Your preoccupation with your new business is important, but will your life partner, and any children you have, feel left out? Some partners describe a new business as a mistress, taking the person they love away from them. Do not lose sight of the need to spend time with your significant others. Remember that there are few business disasters as expensive as a divorce.

Danger!

Make time to pause and reflect. Every entrepreneur needs to take regular reality checks.

Red tape and how to avoid getting it wrapped round your neck

Bureaucracy in all its shapes and forms can appear to be a minefield when you start a business. There are literally thousands of regulations, rules and legal obligations that have the potential to impact on your success.

By following a few simple rules of your own, you will manage to keep red tape in check and not find yourself drawn into a morass of regulatory paperwork. The fact is that some regulations are more important than others and not everything will apply to your business. Ask yourself the following questions.

Am I at risk of breaking the law?

In general, the law relating to you as an entrepreneur is the same as the law relating to you as a citizen. The difference is that, as an entrepreneur, you have more opportunity to break the law and to do it on a greater scale. Do not be tempted in any shape or form.

As an entrepreneur you are legally responsible for the things that your business and particularly any employee does. In other words, if your employee is injured at work, you will be considered at fault. The same applies if a customer is injured by a faulty product. You can get more information about this by talking to:

→ an independent business adviser – for example, from Business Link;

→ membership organisations that represent small businesses – for example, the Federation of Small Business (**www.fsb.org**);

→ trade associations representing businesses in your sector.

Am I at risk of losing business?

Your customers are the most important people you have to please. Because the products and services you supply may form an integral part of the products and services your customers, in turn, supply, there will inevitably be legislation with which they will expect you to comply. A good example of this would be the supermarkets that need documentary evidence that the food products they buy have been transported within a very specific temperature range. Each consignment will be accompanied by a printout from the truck's chiller unit.

Another example is if you supply services to the public sector. They will expect you to have written policies that demonstrate that you are up to date with employment, diversity and other legislation. This protects them from criticism by their stakeholders.

You can get more information by talking to:

→ your customers and potential customers;

→ trade associations representing businesses in your sector.

Am I at risk of losing money?

Arguably, the biggest risk of losing money, apart from trading, is from incurring uninsured losses. These can occur because:

→ you forgot to insure your car for business use and had an accident on the way to a client;

→ your house was burgled and your office computers are excluded from your household policy;

→ a customer slips and breaks a leg, then sues you and you do not have public liability insurance.

Get more information by reading on.

Insurance – dos and don'ts

Nobody likes buying insurance and one of the truest adages in the business world is that 'no one has endurance like a man who sells insurance.' Insurance is difficult to sell and can be annoying to buy; you only see the value when you have to make a claim.

The insurance that you buy for your business will clearly depend upon the business you're in. To find out what you need, talk to a specialist business insurance broker. Alternatively, often you can buy discounted specialist business insurance through trade and membership organisations. These are particularly useful for the kinds of cover the highstreet brokers rarely arrange – for example, professional indemnity insurance which you will need if you provide advice in any shape or form.

When buying business insurance, do:

→ make sure you have the basics covered from day one – including public liability, employer liability (if you have employees), vehicle, premises, contents and stock;

→ shop around and talk to more than one broker;

→ negotiate monthly premium payments rather than 12 months in advance;

→ get the 'need to cover' risks covered first and worry about the 'nice to cover' risks later.

But don't:

→ buy insurance to cover more obscure risks without careful considera-tion – for example, your accountant might suggest you buy insurance that would cover their fees should you be subject to a tax investigation;

→ forget that your bank will probably try to sell you insurance as well – because they will need life cover for security on any borrowing, and also your bank manager will have a sales target to reach. (You can often negotiate an additional period of free banking when you buy insurance from your bank).

Toolkit

The Association of British Insurers is the trade association representing UK insurance companies. It has some useful guides to business insurance at **http://www.abi.org.uk/Display/default.asp?Menu_ID=1141& Menu_All=1,946,1141** or at **http://tinyurl.com/ac6bn6**.

Danger!

Don't let yourself be talked into more life or critical illness insurance than you feel you need or can afford. These policies pay the broker far higher commission rates and understandably are popular things for them to sell.

How to Start Your Own Business for Entrepreneurs

> There are worse things in life than death. Have you ever spent an evening with an insurance salesman? WOODY ALLEN

Intellectual property

Many of us dream of inventing or developing something that we can market exclusively and make a lot of money from. If you have created something completely new, you need to protect it from being copied by competitors. You do this by patenting the product.

Patents, trademarks and copyright are very specialist areas. You need specialist advice particular to your situation. A good place to start is with the UK government's Intellectual Property Office. Their website at **www.ipo.gov.uk** allows you to search existing patents and contains lots of useful advice.

If you are developing something that you think you might need to protect in the future, you can often get development grants from your local and regional development agency. You can find out more about these by talking to your local Business Link.

There are two key points to remember about intellectual property. The first is a practical point. You cannot patent something you have told people about. When you speak to a business adviser or patent attorney they will sign a 'non-disclosure' agreement, which means you can discuss it with them.

The second point is more pragmatic. Patenting an invention does not stop someone from copying it. What it does is enable you to take them on in court and stand a very good chance of winning your case. Remember that litigation can be very time consuming and expensive.

Danger!

If there's no market then there's no point in protecting intellectual property. The value is in it's potential.

Frequently asked questions

The following are questions that may be raised by new entrepreneurs after reading this book about the risks involved in starting a business.

You say that it is important to protect your health when you start a business, but my health is already poor as I live with a disability. Does this mean I should not start a business?

On the contrary, you should start a business because you have a disability. Creating your own work environment enables you to tailor work and lifestyle uniquely to meet your personal needs. Just because you find something is more difficult than others, so, too, will there be things that you find far easier. Choose a type of business that works for you and enjoy success.

Much of the work I plan to do is commissioned by public sector organisations. The paperwork they need as part of the pre-qualification for the tendering process is daunting to say the least. I am not sure where to start. Where would you begin?

I would begin as a subcontractor to a larger organisation that is already active in this field and working with these organisations. This will enable you to build a reputation with the service commissioners, without having to jump through all the compliance hoops you are describing.

Of course, you will earn less than if you contracted direct, but initially you will probably win more work as a subcontractor than by trying to tender and work direct yourself. You can fill in those forms later, when you are better established and more likely to be successful.

I am something of an inventor and have created what I believe is a world-changing product, which will revolutionise the way people work in my industry. As you say, patenting my product is a long and expensive process. How can I be sure it will be worthwhile?

The answer is simple: you need to research your market. The more evidence you have that your product really is going to revolutionise your industry, the more confidence you will have when it comes to spending money. Don't forget to talk to your local regional development agency about development grants to help you take the product to market.

Even if you start out as a one-person business, the time may come when you hire employees. The next chapter will show you how.

Key points

→ Look after yourself as well as your business.

→ Stay legal and buy insurance to cover the most important risks.

→ Protecting your inventions and designs can be expensive. Make sure there is a market first.

Next steps

What action will you take to apply the information in this chapter? By when will you do it?

_____

_____

_____

_____

Your first employee – how to take this giant leap

Chapter Twenty-three

Many entrepreneurs will tell you that taking on their first employee was far more difficult than they had imagined. That's not surprising when you realise that what you are doing by taking someone on is doubling your workforce.

What's more, as the business founder, you need little management and no motivation from anyone else. You have taken some risks and are looking forward to reaping the rewards. You have developed the mindset of an entrepreneur.

Your first employee is also taking a risk. They are joining a young business to do a job that no employed person has done there before. Both you and the person you hire will want the business to succeed, but at times both of you will find things tense and perhaps even traumatic.

You as a new employer will be very aware of the cost of your employee. Every minute that they are not hard at work will seem to you like an hour. You will also need to be both their boss and their work colleague at the same time. You will inevitably be working closely together yet must also maintain some distance.

If you want creative workers, give them enough time to play. JOHN CLEESE

When is the right time to hire someone to help?

There is no secret formula for deciding exactly when the right time is for your business to become an employer. Every business situation is different, and while some will want to work all the hours these are before 'giving in' and sharing the workload, others will be happy to delegate as soon as possible.

Hiring someone is not for the short term. It is a long-term commitment – financial, contractual and, not least, emotional. Your early employees will be buying into your vision and placing great faith in your ability to maintain and grow the business. That is a great responsibility for you to take on.

Conversely, your employee will put their own interests ahead of yours. They are working for a fixed rate of pay. At times, certainly early on, they might even be earning more than you. But later, when your investment in their time begins to pay off, they will be very aware that your earnings are growing quickly.

It is probably the right time to take on your first employee when:

→ you are confident the workload will continue to grow;

→ work is profitable enough to justify it;

→ your goal is to continue to grow the business;

→ there are specific tasks and responsibilities that together will make up an interesting and worthwhile job.

Of course, some businesses need a staff from day one. For example, if you are running a taxi company you will need taxi drivers. If this is you, then you need to be confident that the work is there for the people you recruit from the very beginning. Starting a business with people on the payroll means:

→ your overhead costs will be higher per month;

→ you will need to have the time to manage effectively both the business and your employees.

Time saver

When considering taking on employees, look at recruitment advertising placed by other businesses similar to your own. See what jobs they offer and how. There is no point in reinventing the wheel. Potential employees will be comparing your ads with those of others.

Case study

Jack Smith, Mediaroots, www.mediaroots.co.uk

An entrepreneur from the age of 13, Jack Smith launched Mediaroots with a business partner, Ryan Falconer, when he was 19. His company produces and markets multimedia software training DVDs. The concept grew out of Ryan's MSc dissertation.

Product development and production are outsourced to a team of highly skilled freelancers, who are all much older than Jack. I asked him how he recruits and manages people.

'The internet is amazing and provides effectively a mask or alias to work behind. There is no racism, sexism or ageism unless you want there to be,' he explained. 'People work with me and formulate in their head an image of who they think they're speaking to. The same is true of conducting business on the phone. People talk to me extensively and then find out maybe a few weeks later my age, and are like, 'Wow, I thought I was speaking to a 35-year-old.'

Try before you buy

Before you take on your first employee, often it makes sense to get temporary or short-term help. Such help means you can deal quickly with the heavy workload that confronts you. Recruiting any employee takes time. In fact, if the person you appoint is currently working for someone else, it might be three months between you placing your job advert and your new person starting work.

Not only does taking on temporary help get you the support you need faster, but also it gives you the opportunity to experiment a little with the job role and description before you appoint someone full-time. There are several ways to find short-term help.

Temps

There are many agencies that provide temporary staff or regular part-time staff. The agencies employ the people they place on what is called a zero hours employment contract. This means they are employed, but there is no commitment to give them any work.

When you need help, you call the agency and they will provide you with people with the right skills and experience to do the job. The agency invoices you and in turn pays the temps. You do not have to be involved with your temporary workers' tax, National Insurance or holiday pay. Nor do you have to worry if the work dries up and you have to let them go.

The agency charges you a higher hourly rate than it pays the worker. For example, let's say you run an events business and need security, bar and waiting staff whenever you have an event to run. Working with an agency means you can hire the staff you need when you need them, and if the people you usually have are not available, the agency will find others.

Consultants

Consultants are freelance workers who will work for you on a project basis. Although you are probably thinking about management consultants, they can be IT specialists, telesales professionals, market researchers, translators or almost anything else you can imagine and might need. Most people working in this way are simply good at their job and prefer the freedom and flexibility of self-employment.

Many people who have taken early retirement and want to stay active in their professional field also work as consultants.

You can find consultants and freelancers by:

→ searching business networks, both online (e.g. **www.ecademy.com**) and offline (e.g. Chambers of Commerce);

→ posting projects on specialist online freelancer websites, such as **www.peopleperhour.com**;

→ asking people you know to recommend someone;

→ asking your business adviser – Business Link, for example, maintains a database of consultants with a wide range of skills.

Time saver

Before looking for freelance help, write a very specific project brief that details what has to be achieved. That way you can brief the freelancer properly and, more importantly, measure the success of the project.

What's involved in becoming a boss?

Being a boss means achieving things through other people's efforts and activities rather than your own. The single biggest challenge you face is to let go and delegate things that you have been doing yourself up to now.

In fact, of all the skills you need as a manager of people, the ability to delegate is perhaps the hardest to acquire. You want your employee to do a good job and have hired them to do just that. But do not underestimate how difficult it is to stand by and watch them do something that you know you could do better and faster yourself.

Apart from delegating, or learning to delegate, there is much more involved in becoming a boss. You will also have the following responsibilities:

→ Making sure that the workplace is safe and complies in all respects with health and safety legislation.

→ Providing training and support to make sure that your workers are efficient and effective. This means knowing what skills are needed and assessing people's competencies and working with them to plug any gaps.

→ Having the cash flow to pay them on time and also to pay the associated tax and National Insurance.

→ Making sure you have time to manage your team. No longer can you become totally immersed in your work; you now have to supervise the work of others, too.

 ## Don't keep a dog and bark yourself.

SIXTEENTH CENTURY ENGLISH PROVERB

How to recruit and get it right first time

Although most people have been hired and perhaps promoted in the course of their lives, it is often only when you start your own business that you find yourself recruiting and appointing others.

You will find that, however many job interviews you have attended as a candidate, being the employer in that situation is very different. There are some steps you can follow to get it right first time.

Define the job

First, you have to define the job. It needs a job title and a purpose.
Work out what it is that you need done. Ask others who know you and
your business well what they think the job should entail. Note that this
gets easier the bigger your team becomes.

Benchmark it against others

Next, compare the job with others. Look at similar positions in other
businesses. See how the job is described and how much others are
paying for the same skills. Don't be afraid to look outside your particular industry. Get a feel for the scale of the job and its impact. Finally,
work out how much you think the person will cost and what return on
that investment you will get.

Danger!

The cost of employing someone is considerably higher
than their salary. National Insurance, equipment, training
and the cost of recruitment itself will add between 25 per
cent and 50 per cent to the salary cost. If you pay
someone a salary of £25,000 a year, they will cost you
more than £30,000 a year in total.

Write a job description and person specification

The job description is your opportunity to list the various responsibilities
the new person will have. Look at other job descriptions to see how to

present yours. Most have a list of basic accountabilities and then make clear that the person will also be responsible for anything else they are reasonably asked to undertake.

You will describe the experience, knowledge and skills you are looking for. Remember that when recruiting, you can legally base your choice of candidate only on the person's suitability for the job. You cannot select on grounds of age, gender, race, sexual orientation, and so on.

Decide how to recruit

There are a number of ways you can find people interested in working for you. Each is summarised below and each has its strengths and weaknesses. The route, or combination of routes, you choose will depend on your specific situation.

Advertising
Most newspapers and trade magazines carry recruitment advertising. This is the most open way to recruit and will enable anyone looking for a job to find you easily. The most successful recruitment ads are clear, honest, realistic and state the salary range for the job.

Agency
Agencies will have candidates on their books who are looking for a job and will also advertise. An agency can be good if you do not want others to know that you are recruiting. Often an agency will also short-list, saving you the trouble of doing it yourself. Agencies earn their money by charging a percentage of the first year's salary as a fee. Initially this can be expensive, but compared with the cost of advertising and your time in shortlisting, an agency can work out cheaper. Agencies also have more experience of recruitment and will be able to advise you about the job itself.

Networking
There is nothing wrong with adding to your interview shortlist someone you have met through someone you know. However, recruiting by networking is rarely the best way to find the right person for the job if you

are only looking for one or two people. For highly specialised jobs where there are few people with the necessary skills, though, networking can work well.

Poaching

It is not unusual for people to poach staff from rival firms. This happens a lot in sales teams, where the individual's customer list can seem very attractive. Poaching can lead to disappointment as you never really know how a marketplace will respond to you taking someone from a competitor. Remember that it is important that your company is different from your rivals.

At last, Mr Grimsley felt he'd found the supervisor who would instil discipline into his staff.

Interview

When you interview people it is important that you cover all the points that are relevant to the job. The job description can be a useful document to use to steer the conversation. Use plenty of open questions to get each candidate talking about themselves and what they think they can contribute to your business's success.

If you are not an experienced interviewer and have someone connected with the business (even as an adviser) who can interview alongside you, ask them to do so. Two heads are always better than one in an interview situation and you will find it useful to observe and think while your colleague is interviewing.

Work out the key questions you want to ask before the interview and ask each candidate the same questions. Make the interview as relaxed as possible. People do not perform at their best when feeling pressured (and that goes for you as well as the candidates).

If you work from home, it is worth hiring a hotel room in which to conduct your interviews. It will appear more professional if you interview in a neutral environment.

Offer

If one of the people you interview is, in your view, ideal for the job, you will want to make them an offer. Most jobs are offered on the basis of three months' probation. In other words, you have the option after three months to part company or make their appointment permanent. Remember that it is as much your responsibility as your employee's to make it work.

The best way to offer someone a job is as follows:

→ Conduct a second interview with the most likely one or two people and at that interview discuss salary, training and some of the other practical aspects of the job.

→ Telephone your chosen candidate to ask whether they will accept the job if it is offered. Congratulate them and thank them for their enthusiasm so far. Discuss starting dates and offer support if they have to resign from their current job. Follow up with a letter confirming your offer. You can find examples of job offer letters on business support websites.

→ Make the offer conditional on satisfactory references, if you feel that would be helpful. Referees have a legal obligation to tell you the truth, but it is unlikely you will learn much from references that you have not worked out yourself in getting to know the person.

Time saver

If no one feels suitable, re-advertising and continuing the search may, in the long run, cost you less time than compromising and having to start over after three months. Follow your instincts – they will rarely let you down.

How to Start Your Own Business for Entrepreneurs

The first day

When your new employee joins you on their first day in your company, you have just one chance to make the right first impression. It is the small things that will make the biggest difference. Make sure you have prepared and tidied the area where the new person will work. Make them feel welcome and have enough time set aside to take them through a proper induction into your business and their new job.

Discuss and agree with them on their first day a proper induction programme. List the things that you need to tell them, show them and do. Work through the list with them and add to it things that they might suggest that you have overlooked. Make sure you introduce them to people they will meet and need to know – for example, colleagues and key suppliers.

Danger!

It is important to be friendly with your employees but never to become close friends. You need to maintain a professional distance so that you can remain objective. There will also be things that you cannot tell them because they are confidential to those who own and manage your business.

Danger

Frequently asked questions

The following are some of the questions that new entrepreneurs might raise regarding hiring employees.

I like the idea of using freelance staff rather than employing people. Then I can hire and fire as I need and never have more people around the place than I need. Why would I want to employ someone on a permanent basis?
For one thing, how will you maintain quality with a high turnover of people working in your company? If you show no commitment to them, why should they show you commitment in return? A better policy might be to have some permanent staff and then use temps and freelancers at times of peak demand. You can then make your permanent staff responsible for supervising the temps.

I have worked on my own now for three years and am pretty open and friendly. I'm not sure how employing someone and keeping things to myself will work. Perhaps employing people is not for me. What do you think?

Employing your first member of staff is probably the biggest challenge you have faced so far or will face for some time to come. It is the very conundrum you describe that stops businesses growing. Without hiring staff you can only do the work you can do yourself. It might be that you will be happier on your own than with a team. Only you know the answer to that question.

You haven't mentioned recruitment websites such as Monster.com. Do you think they can be effective?

It all depends on what you are looking for and where in the country you are. There is no harm in trying online recruitment websites as well as other media.

Managing employees will be just one of your day-to-day responsibilities. The next chapter explores some others and shows you how to handle them as effectively as possible.

Key points

→ Work out what you really want before you start recruiting.

→ Consider using freelancers/temps initially to fine-tune the role.

→ Don't look for people like yourself. Look for people whose skills and experience complement your own.

→ If you're daunted by the thought of interviewing, find someone more experienced to help. Explain who they are to the candidates.

→ Once you've offered someone a job, you must follow through and deliver what you have promised.

Next steps

What action will you take to apply the information in this chapter? By
when will you do it?

_____

_____

_____

_____

How to manage your business day to day

Chapter Twenty-four

Running a business is rather like driving a car. You know where you are heading and are out on the road steering your way through the traffic. In front of you is the car's dashboard. This shows how fast you are going, as well as warning you if you run low on fuel or if the engine starts to overheat. You won't be surprised to have learned that large companies have corporate dashboards. These are single-screen summaries of all the statistics that make up the company's performance. It gives senior managers a brief overview, enabling them to spot quickly anything that is going off track .

You are running a small company by comparison. It is unlikely you will have or require the sophisticated, integrated software systems needed to create a corporate dashboard. But it is equally important that you keep your finger firmly on your new venture's pulse. The numbers might be low, but it is your money, reputation and livelihood at stake.

Although right now you might find that the back of the proverbial fag packet provides sufficient space for management information, this will quickly change as your business grows. It makes sense to be an organised manager from day one.

 Management by objectives works if you first think through your objectives. Ninety percent of the time you haven't. PETER DRUCKER

What is management really all about?

Management is nothing more than the process by which you make sure things get done. As Peter Drucker says, management without objectives is difficult. The fact is that you have to know what you want to achieve before you can begin to plan to achieve it.

In a large organisation the leaders will define the objectives and then delegate to the managers the task of achieving them. Each senior manager will break down their share of those objectives into tasks for each of their subordinates, who in turn break it down further. This process means that everyone is working towards the same objectives. Clearly defined departmental and job roles means there is no overlap or duplication.

As an entrepreneur running your own business, you are both a leader and a manager. Until your business grows to the point where you can hire managers to run it for you, you have to wear both hats.

Danger!

If you spend all your time on managing your business and neglect to lead the organisation, it will go nowhere. The danger of becoming too busy working *in* your business to work *on* your business is well known. Make time for both.

Case study

Andy Smith, Corkscrew Events,
www.corkscrcwevents.com

Andy Smith and Mark I inton served together in the British Army and then went their separate ways. A few years later they met again and decided to pool their skills and resources and start a business.

Both had experience of running events and felt that there was an opportunity to set up an events business in the Midlands. Most such businesses seemed to be London-based. They also run their own very successful event, 'The Business Growth Show', throughout the UK.

Success brought with it management challenges. How do you keep your finger on the pulse when the business is growing fast? Andy and Mark realised they were not accounting experts and so hired a good financial controller. They meet weekly to review key performance indicators and translate these into simple, specific goals for their growing team. They also have a mentor, an experienced entrepreneur, to help them stay on track.

Understanding key performance indicators and how to use them

Key performance indicators are the ratios and statistics that in a large organisation might be neatly presented in a corporate dashboard.

The starting point for defining these is your business plan. It will state the activities that you're going to undertake for which you will be paid. Your cash flow forecast should predict the flow of money in and out of the business month by month. Together they contain performance figures that you expect to achieve and therefore need to monitor.

For example, imagine that you have a business offering flights in a hot air balloon. The business is seasonal and you charge per passenger, with a minimum charge for three or less in the basket. Key performance indicators to watch in this situation might include:

→ the number of flights per month;

→ the average number of passengers per flight;

→ customer satisfaction;

→ the ratio of enquiries to bookings;

→ how much money you are owed;

→ the maintenance schedule for your balloon and equipment;

→ employee efficiency and performance.

By regularly recording your firm's performance against each of these key performance indicators, comparing the actual figure with the target, you can quickly see where you are exceeding your business plan forecast or falling behind it. That is the secret of effective management.

Things to measure and things that measure themselves

Every business is different and so will need to monitor different performance indicators. Some you will need to measure, recording what happens and then using a spreadsheet to compare performance against target. Others, like your bank balance, measure themselves, but you still need to monitor them and compare them with your plan. Lastly, some you will measure yourself and others you might well delegate to someone else – for example, your book-keeper. The key performance indicators for your business might include the following.

Money

Everyone monitors their bank balance. From Chapter Twenty-one you know to keep an eye on creditor and debtor days as well. Another indicator you might watch is the extent to which your customers are paying by credit card as opposed to cheque. With credit cards you pay the card company a small commission but have the money in your bank account immediately. As your business grows, you might find it beneficial to encourage more of your customers to pay by credit card to keep your overdraft within the limit. Because you are measuring what is happening, you have the opportunity to influence it.

Customers

Categorising your customers and measuring the spend per customer in each category enables you to work out who your best customers are. For example, if you run a restaurant you might find that business diners spend more freely than young couples out on a date. Because you are measuring this, you know to adjust your marketing to focus more on recruiting business customers than young couples.

If you sell business to business, you will inevitably have a sales pipeline. This contains the people with whom you are building a relationship that have yet to convert to customers. It might take 100 sales enquiries to generate 50 proposals, of which only 20 turn into firm orders. By monitoring these ratios you know the number of enquiries you need to create one sale, and you can also work to improve the conversion rates.

Processes

If you operate business premises, particularly if you make things, you will want to monitor the efficiency of your production processes. Things you might keep an eye on include the physical efficiency of machines, in terms of energy consumption per unit produced. You might also note maintenance and breakdowns so that you can identify where problems are occurring most and deal with the cause.

Finally, you will want to measure your raw material costs and the efficiency with which they are converted into finished products. More expensive raw materials might actually cost less if they lead to more output and less waste.

People

If you employ people, they will probably form the biggest cost. Without becoming overbearing you want to record their efficiency and performance. In a large organisation sick leave and absenteeism might be important statistics to record. In your organisation you might be more interested in people's productivity and their ability to generate positive customer feedback.

Benchmarking

This could be a topic for a book in itself. Benchmarking is the way to measure your performance against that of others in similar situations. Some trade associations collect key performance indicators from their members and then publish them as a league table. Your competitors are not identified but you can see how your performance compares. Most importantly, benchmarking pushes you to improve your performance because you can see what is possible and has already been achieved by others.

Case study
Elaine Clark, Cheap Accounting,
www.CheapAccounting.co.uk

Elaine Clark set up Cheap Accounting in 2007. She's been a chartered accountant for more than 20 years. She saw that there was an opportunity to change the way that accountants work with small businesses by embracing the internet as part of the accounting practice toolkit.

Her clients input their own transactions via a web portal and this enables Elaine to constantly monitor how they are doing. She is proactive, anticipating client needs and sending email updates and fact sheets.

Most client contact is by email, which enables Elaine to keep her cost base low. Her clients are mostly start-ups that welcome an affordable service. By encouraging them to keep their books up to date, she can quickly see where her help is most needed.

Busy fools: how to spot them and how to avoid being one

'Busy fools' are people who have lots to do but never seem to get anything done. They might have lots of customers, do lots of business and never have time to relax, but they never have any money to spend either.

We all know people who are 'busy fools' and, if we are honest, at times we have all been there, too. By measuring the performance of your business carefully you will know what pays and what does not. You will know what makes a profit and what just ties up your time.

Time saver

Make time to measure the performance of your business. If you cannot find the time to do this, you need to do it all the more.

Motivating your new team: steps to success

The benefits to you of monitoring and adjusting the performance of your business are obvious. The benefits to the people you employ will be less obvious. Unless you involve them in some way, working for you will simply be just another job with hours to work and wages to earn.

As you employ people, you will need to set them achievable targets so that they know what is expected of them. You should also discuss and agree any training needs necessary for them to develop the skills and efficiency to achieve the targets. The more you involve your employees in making decisions about how their jobs are done, the better motivated they will be to do them.

People who choose to be employees are motivated by different things from people who choose to be employers. That is a fact that should not be ignored. Good ways to motivate your employees might include:

→ agreeing targets and modest performance bonuses;

→ letting the employees choose when there are two equally productive ways to do something;

→ not judging them by things they cannot influence (it can be easy to blame your staff for things for which you or your customers are responsible);

→ remembering that short-term goals and small rewards are more motivating than long-term goals and large rewards.

Frequently asked questions

Here are some of the questions that new entrepreneurs ask about the day-to-day operation of their businesses.

I'm a one-man band and fly my business by the seat of my pants. Why should I bother with setting and monitoring targets?
I can think of two good reasons. The first is that if, for example, you break a leg and have to hire someone in to do the work, how will you measure it? The second is that you will surely become more proud of your business if you measure its performance and perhaps benchmark against others.

We are setting key performance indicators and are surprised to find that what we thought of as extras are actually where we make a profit. How can we change this to make a profit on everything we do?
Well, maybe you can't. Maybe like some of the budget airlines, you will not make your money from the core activity but from all the peripheral products and services you can sell to your customers on the back of it. What's important is that

you don't do things that you don't need to do and that you make a profit from the whole business.

I like the idea of busy fools. What would be wrong with finding some and keeping them busy as subcontractors doing work for me? Surely this would be very profitable.

It would not be profitable. Busy fools tend to make mistakes more than the rest of us because they are so busy and inefficient. A better route for you to take would be to help some of these people become more efficient and profitable and still make money using them as subcontractors.

As you continue to build up your business, you will also want to build its value. The next chapter will guide you through that process.

Key points

→ Measure the things that matter to your business.

→ Be disciplined and make time to do this.

→ If you find it difficult, find someone to help who finds it easy.

→ Don't be a busy fool.

Next steps

What action will you take to apply the information in this chapter? By when will you do it?

_____

_____

_____

_____

Looking ahead

Part Five

↑

Building value into your business

Chapter Twenty-five

There is a point at which a business takes on a life of its own. It is no longer just you working away on your own and living from hand to mouth. Word has spread and the business has a reputation. Customers are starting to come back and to encourage their friends and associates to use you as well. All of a sudden things are happening without you having to push them.

When this happens to your business, it is starting to acquire real value. The value in a business is in its future potential and not in what has been done before. The more the business is expected to grow and to gain momentum, the more profitable it will be and the more valuable it will become.

One day, when you have recruited the right people, you will find it possible to take time off. In fact, one of the signs of success in growing the business is when you can take a month off and not be missed.

To build value into your business you must invest for the future. You want to enjoy a good income, but rather than taking out every penny you can, it makes sense to use your business as an investment and build it for the future. This is what entrepreneurship is really all about.

 If you would be wealthy, think of saving as well as getting. BENJAMIN FRANKLIN

What is a business really worth?

In short, a business is only worth what someone is prepared to pay for it. You can see how businesses are valued in Chapter Six, which looks at this from the buyer's perspective. Even if you are not considering selling your business, it is worth building in value.

Case study
Simon Campbell, Viapost, www.viapost.com

A serial entrepreneur, Simon Campbell was caught running a flea market in the school playground at the age of ten. Eventually, he moved to Spain to work for a multinational, liked the country and stayed. He's started, built and sold media and software companies. His current company, Viapost, enables customers to dispatch letters straight from their PC to be printed and posted remotely, saving time, money and the environment. It's Skype for mail.

I asked Simon how he adds value to his businesses. 'Obviously, the holy grail is to grow the customer base and tie them in for as long as possible,' he said, 'but there are other ways, also. You need to make it tough for your competitors to use the same routes to market as you.'

When Simon knows he's taken his business as far as he can, he sells it and starts again.

Why is creating value as important as making profit?

The more your business is worth, the more flexibility you have as its owner. Right now, you may not be able to imagine ever wanting to sell it, but one day you might decide that this is the right thing to do. You do not know what the future holds, and one of the benefits of having your own business is having as much freedom as possible to live the life that you want to live.

For example, if you are very successful at competing with a large company, they may well decide to make you an offer. That offer might be significantly higher than the open market value of the business. You could at that point decide to sell, put some money away for your retirement and start a new business from a far stronger base.

Less positive but also possible is that at some point you acquire a health problem that forces you to stop working, or at least restricts your ability in some way. In this situation, if your business has real value, you can sell it or encourage someone to buy in.

Adding value to your business does a lot more than simply making it possible to sell. The other benefits include making it more popular with the following:

→ **Banks**. As your business becomes financially stronger, this will be reflected in its credit rating. Credit ratings are calculated by many factors, including the growth in turnover and the growth in value on the balance sheet. A growing business with manageable debt and a growing balance sheet value will be more attractive to lenders. A business with little or no value will find it harder to borrow money and you as its owner may well be asked to guarantee borrowings.

→ **Large customers**. Your customers will also at times credit-check your company. They want to know that you are strong and able to stay the course. No one likes to do business with a company that looks on the point of collapse. If you are tendering for public sector contracts you often need to submit evidence of your financial strength. This is taken into account when choice of supplier is made. If you are very good at what you do but your business looks weak you may not win work that otherwise would be yours.

→ **Suppliers**. Your suppliers will also credit-check your company. If they do not like what they see, they will not give you credit. Instead, they will ask for cash with order or cash on delivery. Chapters Nineteen and Twenty illustrate why it is important to be able to pay your suppliers as late as you can.

When will this become an issue for me?

Adding value as well as making a profit is an issue you should be addressing from the day you start your business. Inevitably, in the early months, you will be more concerned with building the enterprise and managing cash flow, but you should always have an eye on the importance of building value as well.

As your business grows, its demand for cash will increase. The faster it grows, the greater that demand will be. The more creditworthy your organisation, the easier it will be to find the money you need to do just that.

Remember, too, that you are in business to make money as well as to make a difference in the marketplace you have chosen to inhabit. It is almost inevitable that as you develop your business you will see new opportunities. Sometimes it makes sense to sell what you have and start again, focused on where the greatest opportunity seems to be.

Case study
Simon Wadsworth, The Retail Factory,
www.retailfactory.co.uk

After creating, building and selling several web/digital agencies, it was inevitable that Simon Wadsworth would establish his own e-commerce business. The Retail Factory opened for business in 2007 and plans to be 'the UK's number one online supplier of retail and office supplies'.

Simon sold his earlier companies when approached with a good deal. 'It's difficult to know when it's the right time to sell,' he commented, 'but if the deal looks and feels good, it's probably worth taking.'

Simon also says that the key trick is to put the company in a high profile position when the buying cycle for your type of company turns to you. 'We always spent a lot of money on marketing and PR,' he told me, 'so that our likely buyers were reading about us all the time.'

How do I add value?

All the way through this book there are examples of ways you can add value to your business. Here is a summary to remind you:

→ Make the business less reliant on you by hiring and developing good people.

→ Invest constantly in improving your business's capacity to exceed customer expectations.

→ Specialise in one aspect of what you do rather than trying to be all things to all people.

→ Build customer loyalty so that you can be sure of their continued custom.

→ Protect any intellectual property created by your business.

→ Maintain a positive public profile and build a good reputation.

→ When your accountant has calculated your annual profit, make sure you leave at least half of it in the business to fund future growth.

Case study
Charlie Stockford, Sustain IT Solutions,
www.sustainitsolutions.co.uk

When Charlie Stockford's daughter started at boarding school, Charlie had time to start a new business. A background in both arts and computer software, together with a passion for corporate social responsibility (CSR), led to the creation of Sustain IT Solutions.

The business employs three full-time plus associates and helps large corporate clients evaluate their return on investment in CSR. Clients include tobacco companies and others striving to improve public perception of their products and services.

Charlie's work has enabled her to see that increasingly CSR is an opportunity for small companies, too. In 2009 she rebranded the business and developed a new web-based service that enables even the smallest company to appreciate and measure how important CSR can be for them.

Frequently asked questions

The following are some of the questions that new entrepreneurs may raise regarding building value after reading this book.

I'm confused. Surely it's better to have a high income for many years than a lower income and business with a value?

If you run your business properly you will have both. It is for you and your financial advisers to decide what is right for you, your business and your situation. Remember that the sale of business assets is taxed differently from your income from the business. This is particularly relevant when you get to retirement. In general, I would argue that a business with a high value will also give you a good living and an easy life.

Nowhere in the book do you mention multi-level marketing. I have been offered an opportunity to build a business that will have real value and cost me nothing apart from my hard work to set up. Could you comment please?

Multi-level marketing is certainly a significant and popular route to market for many companies, particularly those selling consumer products. My problem with it is that when it comes to realising the value of the network you have created, you are rather reliant on the parent company. My preference would be to grow a business where I have total ownership and flexibility.

We have had what looks like a generous offer for our business. We were not thinking of selling and were rather taken aback by the approach. Surely, if we have had one offer now, we should hold out and see what else is in the offing? A bird in the hand is worth two in the bush. No one can predict whether the offer you have now is going to be bettered by someone else in the future. My personal goal as an entrepreneur is always to get back what I think is a good return as early as possible. Once I have enough money in the bank to live comfortably on for the rest of my life, I will become more speculative and take bigger risks with what money I have spare. In other words, if I were you I might give the offer serious consideration to see whether it will give you a nest egg and set you up to start a strong business in the future.

In the next, and final, chapter, we'll take a step back to give you a chance to review your goals and decide what part your new business will play in your life.

Key points

→ It is never too soon to start to add value to the business.

→ Value equals choice.

→ A small business is only ever worth what someone is prepared to pay for it.

Next steps

What action will you take to apply the information in this chapter? By when will you do it?

_____

_____

_____

_____

Lifestyle or wealth – a chance to reflect and review your goals

As you have worked through this book, you will have become far more confident in your ability to start and build a successful business. Perhaps you have started your business already and have used this book to fill any gaps in your knowledge, or to cope with the inevitable challenges as they arise.

It is also highly likely that your plans have changed. In fact, as you continue to grow and develop your new enterprise, you will find your plans constantly evolving. This is because the business landscape itself is constantly adapting and changing, forcing you to adapt and change as well. Some see this as a threat but it is a huge opportunity.

This final chapter is here to encourage you to scan the horizon constantly for what is new. It is written also to encourage you to reflect on your personal goals as they change over time, so that your business can deliver them to you. In the final analysis, we all start a business to take control of our lives, and maintaining that control is crucially important.

 Only put off until tomorrow what you are willing to die having left undone. PABLO PICASSO

What have you achieved so far?

Although planning for the future is important, so is recognising what you have achieved to date. It is too easy to forget to enjoy today or celebrate your success so far.

Running a business is rather like learning to ride a bicycle. When you first get on, it seems impossible to balance and make any progress at all. With determination, practise and quite a few bruises, you suddenly master the machine. Soon cycling becomes second nature and you forget how difficult it was in the beginning. Business is just the same.

Once you become confident that your business is on track, you can perhaps begin to look at the bigger picture.

Case study

Andrew Seaton, Resolve IT Solutions,
www.resolvesolutions.co.uk

Andrew Seaton did work experience in a school as part of his university course. He realised that IT support to this sector was poor and vowed to improve it. He also discovered he had a natural aptitude for IT because he enjoyed solving problems.

On graduating, he soon recruited two schools he knew as his first clients and quickly grew the business from there. Now, four years later, his business is established and profitable. It continues to grow, but not at the expense of quality of service.

Andrew has also learned to manage his own expectations and is determined not to become a slave to his company. As he told me, 'I am very lucky that I enjoy my work and find it rewarding, but it's not the be all and end all of life.'

Work/life balance

When you start your business it demands every minute of your time. As it becomes established it remains demanding, but less so than in the early months. This is your opportunity to get your life back in balance. One of the paradoxes of business is that you have the best ideas when you are not at work. It is important to find time to escape from the day-to-day challenges of your business and reflect on the bigger picture. Your family will also appreciate both your company and the opportunity to contribute to your strategic business planning.

Of course, being an entrepreneur is a way of life, but it is very much up to you to make it the kind of life you would like to lead. Here are some examples of ways to help maintain your work/life balance.

→ **Go on a mini-retreat every few months.** This gives you time and space to reflect on your business progress and consider future plans. It could be as simple as a quiet afternoon on the beach with a notebook and pen, or as complicated as a weekend in a monastery where enforced solitude prevents you from being distracted.

→ **Take your family away for the weekend.** Many leading entrepreneurs pick up their best business ideas on holiday. Simply by going somewhere you have never been before and trying things you have never tried before can enable you to see opportunities. Sahar Hashemi, founder of Coffee Republic, wondered why London did not have coffee shops like those she saw in New York. She decided to start her own. You, too, could find inspiration on holiday.

→ **Develop your social life.** An active social life helps you keep your business in perspective. Listening to others talk about their lives, work, challenges and opportunities provides a useful balance for what otherwise might become an obsession. Equally, sharing some of your business experiences with others might prompt obvious questions that you have overlooked.

Danger!

All work and no play will make you less effective.

Longer-term goals

As your business develops over time so, too, will you. Just as your business will mature and age so, too, will you. Whatever age you are now you are inevitably going to get older. Your business is the vehicle you will use to meet your changing needs.

This might sound painfully obvious, but think again. If you are in your twenties you will create a very different kind of business from one you will create in your fifties. Your approach to technology, commerce and life itself will be different according to where you are in your life.

As you go through life your priorities will change. Perhaps you are a single parent fitting your business around your childcare, only able to work part-time, but knowing that in a few years' time you'll want your business to grow so that when you have time to earn more you can do so. Or you might be newly retired and simply wanting your business to keep you occupied and supplement your pension. These people would create two very different businesses, potentially in the same marketplace.

In the same way that you have planned your business, there is also merit in planning your life. Writing a life plan can be a very useful and

How to Start Your Own Business for Entrepreneurs

enlightening exercise. Look at your future ambitions and see where you want to end up. Then you can structure and develop a business to make those things a possibility. Almost anything is possible if you put your mind to it. Listen to your instinct or inner voice. If it feels right, it probably is right!

Frequently asked questions

The following questions reflect some of the concerns entrepreneurs may have regarding the work/life balance highlighted in this book.

I seem to be struggling just to stand still, and at the moment I cannot envisage a time when it would be different. Why end the book with philosophical stuff about long-term goals? I don't think I'll ever get there.

I think you will get there. There is a lot of truth in Maslow's hierarchy of needs. The scientist found that until your basic needs were met you have no interest in what else might be possible. As you build your business you will become more comfortable and better able to look ahead. This short chapter is here to remind you that, however tough today is, if you've worked at your business effectively tomorrow will be better. Here is how Maslow pictured the process:

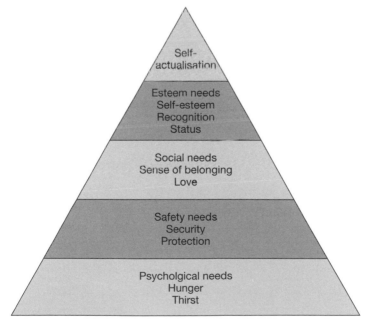

SOURCE: BASED ON MASLOW, A.H. (1943), 'A THEORY OF HUMAN MOTIVATION', *PSYCHOLOGICAL REVIEW*, 50(4) 370-96. THIS CONTENT IS IN THE PUBLIC DOMAIN.

You start at the bottom and over time as each of the needs is met, you see and desire those further up. In business and in life, self-actualisation is the eventual goal.

I have two children and my plan is to create a business that can support them as well as me. I want to build a business that they will inherit and manage. Is that a good idea?
Certainly it is an option, but I would not personally choose to groom my children to take over the family firm. Sometimes it works well and other times it is a disaster. The key seems to be to make sure that your children have wide enough experience of the world of business before they come back to run the family firm. Remember that although you are living the life, you cannot live theirs for them.

Key points

→ Don't overlook what you have achieved already or forget to celebrate each success as it is accomplished.

→ Take time out to reflect on your business and set long-term goals.

→ Acknowledge that as you age your personal goals change and your business goals might need to develop to reflect them.

Next steps

What action will you take to apply the information in this chapter? By when will you do it?

_____

_____

_____

_____

How to Start Your Own Business for Entrepreneurs

Index